Releasing the Spirit of Prophecy

BOOKS BY BILL JOHNSON

A Life of Miracles

Dreaming With God

Face to Face

Here Comes Heaven

Release the Power of Jesus

Strengthen Yourself in the Lord

The Supernatural Power of a Transformed Mind

When Heaven Invades Earth

AVAILABLE FROM DESTINY IMAGE PUBLISHERS

Releasing the Spirit of Prophecy

BILL JOHNSON

DESTINY IMAGE® PUBLISHERS, INC.
P.O. Box 310, Shippensburg, PA 17257-0310

"Promoting Inspired Lives."

This book and all other Destiny Image, Revival Press, Mercy Place, Fresh Bread, Destiny Image Fiction, and Treasure House books are available at Christian bookstores and distributors worldwide.

Previously published as *Release the Power of Jesus*
For more information on foreign distributors, call 717-532-3040.
Reach us on the Internet at www.destinyimage.com.

ISBN 10: 0-7684-0481-9
ISBN 13: 978-0-7684-0481-4

For Worldwide Distribution, Printed in the U.S.A.

1 2 3 4 5 6 7 8 9 10 11 / 17 16 15 14

Dedication

I dedicate this book to my children and their spouses—Eric and his wife, Candace; Brian and his wife, Jenn; Leah and her husband, Gabe. They amaze me. They have embraced the call of God to *re-present* Jesus to the world through the lifestyle presented in this book. I am blessed by their hearts for God and their approaches to life. And I pray that the inheritance of God's mighty works will multiply in their hands. To all six of you—*I love you!*

Acknowledgments

Allison Armerding—You did a great job of taking my materials and putting much of it into a readable form. again. Again, thanks.

Dann Farrelly—Your skills at editing content and flow of information have helped me beyond words. It is an honor to partner with you for the Kingdom. Thanks.

Pam Spinosi—Your help in editing is priceless. Thanks.

Mary Walker—Your help in gathering information and helping with the process of writing a book have been invaluable to me. Thanks.

Endorsements

Bill Johnson has done it again! He has written a wonderful book that will build your faith, activate you to another level in the supernatural and a book that could be a catalyst for another healing revival. I highly recommend this life-changing book!

Che Ahn
President and Founder of Harvest International Ministry

When Bill Johnson begins to tell the testimonies of what God is doing through people in his school or church, or the testimonies of what God is doing in his ministry, it is always a highlight in our Schools of Healing and Impartation or conferences. You can feel faith building in the room and sense the electricity increasing in the room with the power of Heaven when the testimony is being told. Now in Bill's newest book, *Releasing the Spirit of Prophecy,* you too can experience the power of these testimonies. I know you will be encouraged and will expect greater miracles in your life, your church, and your work than ever before. The power is in the testimonies whether you hear them or read them; get them into your renewed mind.

Randy Clark
Founder of Global Awakening

Author Bill Johnson is not only a pioneer but also a practitioner of the Kingdom of God with more than twenty years of experience in explaining, expressing, and expanding the implications of the Kingdom.

The loudest and clearest *amen* on the vital truths herein as well as in his other previous volumes continues to be sounded and observed from Bethel Church, Redding, California, a veritable laboratory of Kingdom training and activity.

Because of this book, I will never be able to view the word *testimony* in the same narrow sense as I viewed it before. It will bring readers to the clear terms of why we must and how we can release the power of God to bring order amid the chaos of the 21st century.

Jack Taylor, President
Dimensions Ministries
Melbourne, Florida

I have worked with Bill Johnson for more than 30 years and have never known anyone who walks in more integrity and intimacy with God than Bill does. He is one of those rare individuals in life whom the more you get to know him, the more you admire him. This book, *Releasing the Spirit of Prophecy,* is not only a great book that will activate you in supernatural ministry, but is also a rare look into the life of a man who is a friend of God. In this book Bill teaches us how to develop a culture in us, through us, and around us that invites a holy visitation and establishes a habitation for the Kingdom of God so that miracles become a natural way of life. Bill shows us how the impact of the testimony can transform us from mere Christians into modern-day revivalists.

If you are bored, feeling powerless, or living a joyless Christian life, this book is for you. Much like the apostle Peter, you are about to be invited out of the leisure ship and into the stormy seas of the great adventure. Don't look down!

Kris Vallotton
Co-founder of the Bethel School of Supernatural Ministry
Author, *The Supernatural Ways of Royalty*,
Developing a Supernatural Lifestyle, and others

Contents

Preface

My great passion is for reformation. It must happen before Jesus returns, for He is returning for a victorious Bride. This great move of God will impact families, churches, cities, and nations. For that to happen, we must first have an overwhelming sense of God's presence, followed by a deep devotion to truth. This book is an attempt to shape Christian culture with truth that restores us to that which God intended.

I am very excited for the days directly ahead of us. His outpourings are increasing, both in frequency and in demonstrations of power and glory. This is the moment all the prophets spoke of. And this outpouring is to become the move of God that never ends. It's worth living for. And it's worth dying for.

A Prisoner of Promise
Bill Johnson

CHAPTER 1

Truth
Empowers

One day I was sitting in my office reading the Book of Revelation, when I felt something unmistakable—the feeling I get when the words seem to jump off the page and I know I am hearing a present word from the Lord. I thought, *Wow! That is so powerful! I have no idea what it means, but it's powerful!* (As usual, my spirit was getting it much faster than my mind.)

The verse I had read was Revelation 19:10: "And I fell at his feet to worship him. But he said to me, 'See that you do not do that! I am your fellow servant, and of your brethren who have the testimony of Jesus. Worship God! *For the testimony of Jesus is the spirit of prophecy.*'" It was particularly this last sentence that had just exploded in my heart, and I knew it had powerful implications extending far beyond the context of John's encounter.

For the next few moments I meditated on this phrase, asking the Holy Spirit to help me understand what He meant. A few hours later, the answer walked right through my office door. One of the men in the church, whom I'll call Jim, stopped by to share a testimony of how God had powerfully restored his marriage. After he finished the story he said, "Bill, you have my permission to tell this testimony to anyone you know who needs to hear it."

This statement suddenly connected the dots for me. Testimony and prophecy had always been important elements of the Christian life, but in this moment I realized that this man was telling me that I could *use his testimony to prophesy* over people. (Prophecy either foretells the future or causes a change in the present. A testimony then becomes catalytic in its ability to bring about a change of atmosphere in the present, making room for a supernatural release.)

Jim had instinctively made two assumptions: first, that if God had done this great thing for him, He would surely do it for others; and second, that *declaring the testimony* was the vehicle by which this promise would be transmitted to others in need.

The first assumption is clearly supported in the Scriptures, which state that God is the same yesterday, today, and forever and is no respecter of persons (see Heb. 13:8; Acts 10:34). And the second assumption, I recognized in that moment, was a practical application of the truth that the testimony of Jesus is the spirit of prophecy. Testimonies prophesy God's intent and nature to all who will hear.

A RIPPLE EFFECT

That experience happened 25 years ago. Since then I have intentionally shared testimonies when I minister and have closely observed the results, which have been consistently stunning.

One of my favorite stories to tell is of a little boy who got healed one night at a regional renewal meeting in one of the towns on the Northern California coast where I have ministered on many occasions. At the time he was 3 years old and had fairly severe clubfeet.

I had brought some students from the school of ministry at Bethel Church to the meeting, and they prayed for him. When they set him on the ground, his feet were perfectly flat for the first time. Another little friend of his came up to him and said, "Run!" He immediately took off running.

My wife captured the whole thing on a video. The following week we got to show everyone back at Bethel the footage of this little boy running in a big circle, coming back to the camera saying, "I can run!" It was amazing. Two weeks later his neighbors drove three hours to attend our Sunday morning meeting. When I asked them how the little boy was doing, they told me he had been running for two weeks.

The next day two students from our School of Ministry went down to the local mall to look for people to show God's love to through prayer. This was a normal activity for them. A couple of them noticed an older woman walking with a leg brace and a cane and decided she was a good candidate. They approached her and asked her if they could pray for her. She told them flatly, "No."

Undeterred, they persisted and explained that they had just seen a little boy healed of clubfeet. *After they shared the testimony*, the woman had a change of heart and said they could pray for her. They first prayed for her knee, which had a tumor on it. The tumor disappeared, so the woman removed her brace. Then the Lord showed one of the students, through a word of knowledge, that He was also healing her back and that the fire of God's presence was touching a specific place on her back.

When the student pointed to the exact spot, the woman found that the other tumor had disappeared as well. She had never told them about that one. Right after that happened, her family came out of the store and saw that Grandma had been healed. The woman walked out of the mall carrying her cane and leg brace.

Some time later, I shared these two stories in a Sunday morning service as an illustration of the prophetic power of a testimony. A woman visiting from Montana had a 2-year-old little girl whose feet turned inward so severely that she would constantly trip over them whenever she tried to run. After hearing the testimonies and the teaching, the woman said in her heart,

"I'll take that for my daughter." When she went to pick up her little girl from our nursery, she found that her feet were already perfectly straight. No one had laid hands on her or prayed. It just happened with God's supernatural intervention when her faith was ignited through the power of a story.

More recently, I shared the testimonies of these three miracles in a conference held at Mahesh and Bonnie Chavda's church in North Carolina. The man who drove me between the hotel and the church was from Brazil. As he was driving me back to the hotel after the meeting, he told me that he had just received a phone call from his sister-in-law in Brazil. She had watched that night's service on her computer. When she heard the story about the clubfeet being healed and then heard about the little girl's feet that were turned inward also being healed, she called out to her daughter.

Her little girl was about ten years old. Her feet turned inward so severely that they were actually deformed. She is a beautiful young girl, but when people look at her and they just stare at her feet, it's embarrassing to her. After hearing the teaching on the testimony and the stories that followed, his sister-in-law called to her daughter, who was in another room. She responded, "Yes, Mommy" and came and stood in the hallway. Her mother then told her to take off her shoes. After the girl removed her shoes, the mother told her to come to her. As she walked toward her mother, the feet straightened and were completely healed. Once again, faith was released through the power of a story.

There is no doubt in my mind that these individuals each experienced the prophetic power of the testimony. When they heard the testimony of what God had done, the anointing on the testimony opened a realm of possibility. The atmosphere became pregnant with the opportunity for the miracle that had been described in the testimony to be duplicated. When they engaged their faith and stepped into that opportunity in the slightest measure, that possibility became reality.

In two of these cases, no one even prayed for, laid hands on, or was even present in the room with the person who was healed. And this is just one of *many* stories that connect back to one specific breakthrough miracle. I and other members of my leadership team and church have seen this list of related God's supernatural interventions continue to grow as specific miracles are multiplied through the declaration of a testimony.

One particular series is so prolific and so clearly the result of the testimony that it is overwhelming. It began a few years ago when I was praying for people at a conference in Minnesota. There was a young lady there who had been in a bad accident and injured her leg. She had pins in her leg, pain, restricted movement, and other complications.

As we prayed for her, calcium deposits started to dissolve, she gained more movement, and pain left. When she got up the next morning and got dressed to come to that day's meeting, her husband looked down at her leg and said, "Hey, that wasn't there before." A whole part of her calf muscle that had been destroyed in the accident had grown back overnight. At the meeting she gave the testimony and we all praised God for this creative miracle.

Following her testimony, a woman immediately came up to me and said, "If God would do that for her, certainly He would do that for me." She caught on to what the testimony had just provided for all who really heard it, even though I had not taught on the principle. This woman had severed her Achilles tendon five years earlier. It had never healed correctly, and part of the calf muscle had atrophied and withdrawn up into the leg.

So I had the young lady who had just been healed, as well as the pastor's wife, come and pray for this woman. I told the one recently healed, "Freely you've received, freely give." They laid hands on the woman needing the miracle and watched as God reattached the tendon correctly and redeveloped the muscle right before their eyes.

Then another lady came up while that was going on and said, "Hey, I was kicked in the leg by a horse, and it destroyed part of my calf muscle. There's a growth in its place." So the two ladies who had been healed and the pastor's wife laid hands on her. They watched the growth dissolve and the muscle form right before their eyes.

Another lady came up. It seemed like there was an epidemic of calf muscle injuries in Rochester, Minnesota. She also got healed. The same miracle was duplicated three times in a few moments.

I flew from Rochester to minister in Crossville, Tennessee, where I shared the story of these four women. In the room was a doctor who had broken his leg one year earlier. He had restricted movement and pain, and his whole calf muscle had atrophied. I sent some students to pray for him, and about twenty minutes later I asked, "How are you doing?" He told me that all the pain was gone and all the movement was back. Then I asked, "How is the muscle?" He said, "I can feel the skin stretching."

When I arrived home in Redding from the Crossville meetings I told the testimonies of these five people. There was a woman in the room who had broken her leg a year earlier. She had pain, restricted movement, and an atrophied calf muscle. She came up to me about two weeks later and said, "When you shared that testimony, my leg became hot. All the pain left, I regained full range of motion, and the muscle grew back."

Later, I shared these stories at a signs and wonders ministry training meeting in Brazil. I had gone there to help Randy Clark with his crusades. A woman on the ministry team from the United States was missing part of a calf muscle due to an automobile accident. After I was through with my message, she went to the bathroom to examine her leg. She found that the muscle had grown back while I was teaching.

More recently, I told these stories in another meeting with Mahesh and Bonnie Chavda. A woman in the audience interrupted me as I was sharing them and said, "I'm missing part of a calf muscle." I told her we'd be happy to pray for her after the meeting. Then she said, "And I'm from Minnesota."

Realizing that unusual coincidences are often the language of the Spirit, I understood that this was a divine setup. So I had her run to the back of the room, and then back to where she was sitting—faith needs an activity, whether it is quietly uttering, "I'll take that for my daughter" or calling her into the room and having her walk to you. The muscle was created during her act of obedience to an unusual command.

I never realized that there were so many people missing part of their calf muscles. The Holy Spirit used these unusual experiences to let me know that I needed to sit up and give my full attention to what He was saying about the testimony. In learning how God speaks to us I've also learned that besides unusual coincidences, He also speaks through the spoken or written record (testimony) of anything that God has done. It is how God often speaks to His people. As all of this was unfolding, I couldn't help but feel that God really wanted me to get this, so He was making it *really* obvious.

GOD'S NATURE REVEALED

Initially it seemed like the primary aspect of the testimony that God wanted me to *get* was its value in ministering to people who needed a miracle. But as always, God's acts reveal His ways, and His ways reveal His nature. Thus, the revelation of the power of the testimony has unfolded for me beyond the immediate context of ministry and led me to discover that it is a foundational Kingdom principle with implications for every area of our lives as believers. It is a principle that must be taught, understood, and applied on an individual and corporate level if the Church is going to fulfill her commission to disciple nations through preaching and demonstrating the Gospel of the Kingdom.

What I have discovered is that our ability to fulfill this calling and commission depends largely on one vital thing—remembering. *Our capacity to remember what God has said and done in our lives and throughout history—the testimony—is one of the primary things that determine our success or failure in sustaining a Kingdom lifestyle of power for miracles.*

As we explore the nature of the testimony and the priority of remembering, I believe we will see that the Church must begin to establish core truths and practices in our culture in order to unlock the heavenly resources God has put in the testimony. We must have these resources in order to accomplish all we are called to become and to do, releasing His miracle power into our world.

CHAPTER 2

Spending Our
Inheritance

One of my primary jobs is to teach Christians how to discover and spend their inheritance. This basically means that we learn to use the unlimited promises given to us by God to bring about a manifestation of His dominion for the sake of humanity. It is always recognized through purity and power and is motivated by God's love.

I am convinced that, for the most part, the Church has left the riches of Heaven sitting in the bank, thinking that we only get them when we die and go there. The belief that Heaven is entirely a future reality has reduced far too many of God's declarations in Scripture about the believer's identity and calling to "positional" truths that are acknowledged but never experienced. It is time for that to change.

Understanding our inheritance begins with discovering the deeper purpose for our salvation. Many new believers stay immature because they never progress beyond the revelation that they are sinners saved by grace. By *progress* I don't mean "to leave behind," but "to build upon." Those who progress are those who understand that God's highest purpose for the Cross was not merely to forgive us of sin. It was so that, by forgiving us on the basis of Christ's blood, He could invite us back into an intimate family relationship with Him, our heavenly Father. John 1:12 says, "But as many as received Him, to them He gave the *right* to become children of God, to those who believe in His name." This legal standing of relationship to God as His sons and daughters is precisely what gives us an inheritance. Romans 8:14-17 explains this simply:

> *For as many as are led by the Spirit of God, these are sons of God. For you did not receive the spirit of bondage again to fear, but you received the Spirit of adoption by whom we cry out, "Abba, Father." The Spirit Himself bears witness with our spirit that we are children of God, and if children, then heirs—heirs of God and joint heirs with Christ, if indeed we suffer with Him, that we may also be glorified together.*

The fact that we are *heirs of God* is mind-boggling. But we must not be content to read these verses and be awed by them. They prophesy our potential, a potential that we must pursue throughout our entire lives.

John 1:12 says we have the right to *become* the children of God. When God invites us into relationship with

Him, He is inviting us into a process of becoming, of transformation. This transformation can be measured in our lives because in Jesus Christ we have the model of who we're becoming as the children of God. We see it later in Romans 8:29: "For whom He foreknew, He also predestined to be conformed to the image of His Son, that He might be the firstborn among many brethren." We have the right to become like Christ, our Elder Brother. We are destined to be fully restored to the image and likeness of God, in which we were originally created.

Through salvation we are also restored to our original purpose—the purpose that flows naturally from our restored identity and relationship with God. Ephesians 2:10 says, "For we are His workmanship, created in Christ Jesus for good works, which God prepared beforehand that we should walk in them." Works cannot save us, but without the fruit of good works in our lives, we lack the evidence that identifies us as new creations in Christ. Just as God's nature is revealed in what He does, the evidence that we are being transformed into His likeness is that we reveal His nature in what we *do*.

What are these good works? It's too easy to reduce Jesus' teaching to what is humanly possible. While we love to feed the poor, clothe the naked, and visit those in need (such acts of kindness are essential expressions of the Christian life), we refuse to let them satisfy that internal drive for effective service. He specifically used the term "good works" to describe the miracles, signs, and wonders He performed.

Jesus modeled these works for us. He didn't design a new hearing aid or train a guide dog. He healed the deaf and the blind. This overwhelming conclusion about "good works" comes from a thorough study of the Gospel of John. These good works not only reveal Jesus to be the Anointed One, the Christ; they also reveal the specific nature of His relationship with His Father, as He explained in John 14:8-12:

> *Philip said to Him, "Lord, show us the Father, and it is sufficient for us." Jesus said to him, "Have I been with you so long, and yet you have not known Me, Philip? He who has seen Me has seen the Father; so how can you say, 'Show us the Father'? Do you not believe that I am in the Father, and the Father in Me? The words that I speak to you I do not speak on My own authority; but the Father who dwells in Me does the works. Believe Me that I am in the Father and the Father in Me, or else believe Me for the sake of the works themselves. Most assuredly, I say to you, he who believes in Me, the works that I do he will do also; and greater works than these he will do, because I go to My Father."*

It can't be stated more plainly. Those who believe in Him will demonstrate signs and wonders. But even more so, His declaration implies that those who believe will walk in the same kind of relationship with the Father and possess the same anointing of the Spirit as He did. That is, we are called to minister as Jesus ministered because, through His death and resurrection, we have access to everything He had available to Him to do *good works*. He prophesied this to His disciples and to us when He said, "As the Father has sent me, I also send you" (John 20:21).

COMMISSIONED TO DO THE IMPOSSIBLE

When Jesus commissioned the 12 disciples to go into the world and make disciples of the nations, He was commanding them to do the impossible. Many Christians mistakenly believe that some of Christ's commands, like the command to love your neighbor as yourself, are possible to observe, while others, like the one to raise the dead, are impossible. The truth is that all of Christ's commands are impossible to fulfill apart from His grace and supernatural power through the Holy Spirit. Our heart to obey whatever He says puts us in the place of living from the promise, "All things are possible to him who believes." (See Mark 9:23.) Our faith gives us access to all the resources of Heaven. This is why Christ commissioned us to do the impossible!

We, as sons and daughters of God, are destined to reveal our Father to the world by bearing His likeness. We do this as Christ did, by communing with the Father, walking in the anointing of the Holy Spirit, and bringing the Kingdom of Heaven to earth through demonstrations of power and authority, all in the context of show-ing the love of God.

For this reason, we must learn to spend our inheri-tance by drawing on the great promises of God for the benefit of the people around us. We can't forget that it was Jesus' *death* that allowed the essence of God's *will* to be released to the rest of His family, the saints ("on earth as it is in heaven"). We must not wait until we die to use our inheritance because our purpose on earth requires heavenly resources to fulfill it.

The anointing to heal and bring deliverance will be of no value in Heaven. These graces must be used here and now as part of the package of tools used to bring the nations to Jesus. After all, He is called "the desire of the nations." Everyone desires Jesus. They just don't know it. We must become like Him more fully so that the harvest becomes all that God desires and has provided for.

So then, if our right to become the sons of God gives us *access* to the same kind of relationship that Jesus has with the Father, how do we learn to grow in that relationship? Thankfully, Jesus modeled this for us as well. Jesus did not come out of the womb with an adult mind, fully aware of His identity and destiny. He had to undergo the same process of maturity that we all do. The Scriptures say, "…He learned obedience…" (Heb. 5:8). But He was trained in His relationship with God by at least three things. First, He was trained by the record of God's activities among man as recorded in Scripture. Hebrews 10:5-7 describes how Jesus discovered God's will and His destiny there:

> *Therefore, when He came into the world, He said: "Sacrifice and offering You did not desire, but a body You have prepared for Me. In burnt offerings and sacrifices for sin You had no pleasure. Then I said, 'Behold, I have come—in the volume of the book it is written of Me—to do Your will, O God.'"*

Second, it is highly likely that Jesus was raised under the influence of the testimony of His parents, particularly Mary, who had "treasured" every word, dream, and event that had been spoken or occurred concerning Jesus' conception and birth. It says that she "pondered them in her heart" (Luke 2:19).

Third, Jesus had the testimony of the Holy Spirit, who facilitated Jesus' communication with the Father, "[the Spirit] will not speak on His own authority, but whatever He hears He will speak" (John 16:13). In giving us instruction on the Holy Spirit's role in leading us into truth, He is in fact revealing to us how He has lived. These three resources are all *testimonies*. Testimonies are the things that train you and me to walk in a relationship with the Father and fulfill our purpose as His sons and daughters.

The Psalmist said, "I have inherited Your testimonies forever, for they are the joy of my heart" (Ps. 119:111 NASB). The testimonies of the Lord are our inheritance.

And what is a testimony? *A testimony is the written or spoken record of anything God has done in history.* Everything God has said and done in history is your eternal possession, and that record holds all the resources you need to be transformed into the image of Christ and become a transformer through demonstrating His good works.

The purpose of this book is to try to examine some of the weightiness and power of that inheritance and display it for what it is, namely releasing miracle power.

THE TESTIMONY REVEALS GOD

The first thing to see in the definition is that a testimony is about what *God* has done. When believers hear the word *testimony*, they often associate it with the story of how they came to know Christ, or perhaps a story about someone who experienced a miracle. But we are never the main characters in a testimony. Our stories are testimonies because they tell of what God has done.

The corollary to this statement is also true, that we don't have a testimony unless we have experienced a divine invasion of God in our lives! We are His witnesses only to the degree we have encountered His power. As Acts 1:8 points out, it is after we receive power and the Holy Spirit comes upon us that we are witnesses. A *witness* means "someone with a testimony"; it is the very word Jesus used to describe His true disciples.

The testimonies of God are an invaluable inheritance because in each story of what God has done, there is a revelation of His nature. But giving us a better theology is not the primary purpose of that revelation. A revelation of God through a testimony is *always* an invitation to know God experientially in that revelation.

Such encounters transform us. And transformed people transform people. David knew the heart of the Father as seen in Psalm 40:6-8—the passage quoted in the verses we just saw in Hebrews 10—and understood that they held a revelation of the nature of God. Jesus came to earth knowing that God did not want animal sacrifices and burnt offerings; He wanted a man who would do His will. Jesus embraced His assignment, and it led Him to experience His Father's delight as He fulfilled the Father's desire.

Jesus explained the power source of His ministry when He said, "...Most assuredly, I say to you, the Son can do nothing of Himself, but what He sees the Father do; for whatever He does, the Son also does in like manner. For the Father loves the Son, and shows Him all things that He Himself does..." (John 5:19-20).

This reality is the same source of life and power for every believer. Knowing the testimonies of God is a crucial part of "seeing what the Father does." Experiencing God through what He has done in the past correctly positions us to experience God in what He is doing in the present. The more we come to know God experientially by responding to the invitations in His testimonies, the more we can become like Him. And the more we become like Him, the more we can do what He does and manifest His nature and power to the world around us.

HEAVEN'S RESOURCES

Power is probably one of the first *heavenly resources* that comes to mind when you consider what you need to fulfill your destiny to do the impossible.

Power is a huge part of your inheritance, but the way to walking in power cannot be separated from personally encountering the God of power. You will grow in your relationship with Him through that experience.

The testimonies of God are the key to walking in power because, in unveiling who God *is*, they teach believers to pursue a relationship with Him more than gifts or answers to prayer. God is longing for His people to love Him along with His gifts. He is longing for them to encounter His incredible love so they will be motivated by passion more than duty. Then He can trust them with His power in unprecedented measure.

The anointing that empowers us to be like Christ and do good works is not an impersonal force. The anointing is a Person. It is the Holy Spirit Himself, and He is passionate to accomplish something very specific in us—to conform us to the image of Christ. The more room we make for Him in our lives, the more He puts His power and revelation to work for that purpose. He is the One who reveals what the Father is doing and saying and then equips us to do and say it.

Communication with the Spirit was the secret to Christ's ministry, and it is the secret to ours. The testimonies of God teach us what the Holy Spirit is like and how to move with Him. They keep us aware of the God who invades the impossible when the perspectives of those around us are focused on the temporary, physical circumstances.

Without a constant awareness of God and the testimonies that speak of His nature, we will inevitably reduce our vision and ministry down to what we can accomplish with our gifts and strength. God is obviously the One who gave us these gifts, but they are like sails on a boat, designed to catch His wind. Without the wind of the Holy Spirit filling them, they have no eternal purpose. He comes to direct their course beyond the reach of human possibility. Without God these abilities have no effect on eternity.

HISTORY IS A STORY

The study of the testimony is a study of history, because the testimony is the record of what God has done in the past. In order to understand the power of the testimony, we need to know what *history* contains.

History is more than a series of random events. It is a story with a plot, characters, theme, and an outcome. It has a beginning, middle, and end. We know history is a story because it has an Author. Thus, there may be a thousand different opinions on what history means or where it's going, but there is only one opinion that is true. That's why divine perspective is absolutely necessary for us to understand history, as well as our purpose in the present.

Like a testimony, history is most truly about God, the Author of your story and mine. While He didn't write for tragedy and crises to fill our lives, He did arrange for His solutions to always be at hand. For this reason, history itself *is* a testimony, composed of the collective testimonies of God.

The family of God inherits His testimonies just as members of a royal family inherit their family history. Royals study and rehearse the record of their ancestors because it is their connection to that past that gives them their identity and purpose for their lifetime. It lays on them a responsibility of doing something significant during their reign in order to pass the legacy on to the next generation. If one generation fails to live in such a way that honors their family history or fails to pass that history on to the next generation, that line is broken and the inheritance is potentially lost.

That reality is no less true for us, who have been adopted into the royal family of God. When Christ Jesus purchased us through a payment in blood and brought us from death to life, our history was changed. We were on a trajectory to hell. But after we said yes to Jesus, our entire past, present, and future were brought into the history of God and His people.

The Cross has the power to transform and redeem us so completely that our sinful past becomes a testimony of God's power, bringing Him glory. But we can't walk in that transformation unless we learn to live from our family history. I'm not talking merely about studying the lives of past believers, or even studying Scripture, though those activities are certainly important. But they are important because they teach us God's version of history and help us gain insights on reality from His perspective, which enables us to live supernaturally. Scripture calls this training process *renewing the mind.*

OUR ORIGINAL PURPOSE

Most of us are acutely aware that we live in a world at war. But the war is not over power, land or money, or even good and evil. It is over something even more basic. The war is over truth, and the battlefield is the mind of every person.

This war began in Heaven, when satan was cast down, but we were implicated in it by Adam and Eve—not only when they ate the forbidden fruit, but also when they decided to trust in a lie over God's truth.

Eating the fruit was merely evidence that they had believed the enemy's lie. When you believe a lie, you empower the liar. Agreeing with the devil empowers him—giving him license to kill, steal, and destroy. When Adam and Eve did so, they denied God's truth, which amounted to cutting off the branch on which they were sitting. Adam and Eve literally *fell* when they decided to abandon God's perspective for a distortion. Romans 1:18-21 describes the Fall of Man explicitly as a fall *from the truth*:

> *For the wrath of God is revealed from heaven against all ungodliness and unrighteousness of men, who suppress the truth in unrighteousness, because what may be known of God is manifest in them, for God has shown it to them. For since the creation of the world His invisible attributes are clearly seen, being understood by the things that are made, even His eternal power and Godhead, so that they are without excuse, because, although they knew God, they did not glorify Him as God, nor were thankful, but became futile in their thoughts, and their foolish hearts were darkened.*

Paul says that the reality of God's eternal power and nature are "clearly seen" in the visible realm. That phrase literally means "seen from above." When Adam and Eve fell, they fell from God's perspective on reality. Before they "suppress[ed] the truth," they had unbroken access to the truth of God's nature and His intentions for history.

Paul also says, "What may be known of God [was] manifest in them." This implies that, because they were made in the image of God, they could look at each other and see what God was like. But when they suppressed the truth of whom God was, their own image was distorted, separating them from their identity and purpose. From this point on, the human race inherited a distorted perspective on reality and history.

Now that the breach of sin has been healed by the Cross, believers must allow the testimonies of God to teach us the truth that was lost to Adam and Eve—both His plan for history and our identity and role in it. God's plan for mankind has never changed, because He has not changed. But the Church has not yet understood that plan to the degree that we begin collectively walking in it, I believe, because our minds have not yet been sufficiently renewed by the testimonies of God.

As I mentioned, most believers understand that God has forgiven them of sin, but many haven't entered into the purpose of that forgiveness. When Adam and Eve sinned, God wasn't shocked. He was fully aware of the risk He had taken in giving them free will. He wanted sons and daughters who would love Him, and love requires a choice.

We know He wasn't blown away because He already had a plan to redeem man if they chose to use their free will for something other than love. Revelation 13:8 declares that Jesus is the "Lamb slain from the foundation of the world."

I don't want to minimize the disastrous effects of sin or the immense debt God paid in sacrificing His own Son for us. We truly have a great salvation. It is so great and so complete, because in forgiving us, God purposed for His original plan in history to be accomplished.

We learn this from the testimony of Scripture. When God placed Adam and Eve in the Garden, He commissioned them to be fruitful, multiply, fill the earth, and subdue it (see Gen. 1:28). Two people were not enough to rule the planet. God wanted the earth filled with those made in His image who would bring the earth under the influence of the King and His Kingdom.

When sin entered the world, mankind forfeited that authority to the enemy. For centuries that slavery endured, but God prepared the world for the deliverance that would come through the Messiah with a series of revelations (testimonies).

Virtually all of these revelations, to Noah, Abraham, Isaac, Jacob, and the people of Israel, involved covenants. In the next chapter, I'll explain the fundamental relationship between the testimony and covenant, but here I want to point out a recurring theme in each of these revelations.

To Noah He said, "Be fruitful and multiply on the earth" (Gen. 8:17). To Abraham, He said, "I…will multiply you exceedingly. …I will make you exceedingly fruitful" (Gen. 17:2,6). To Isaac, He said, "I will make your descendents multiply as the stars of heaven" (Gen. 26:4). To Jacob, He said, "Be fruitful and multiply" (Gen. 35:11). And finally to the people of Israel, He said:

> *For I will look on you favorably and make you fruit-*
> *ful, multiply you and confirm My covenant with*

you. You shall eat the old harvest, and clear out the old because of the new. I will set My tabernacle among you, and My soul shall not abhor you. I will walk among you and be your God, and you shall be My people. I am the Lord your God, who brought you out of the land of Egypt, that you should not be their slaves; I have broken the bands of your yoke and made you walk upright (Leviticus 26:9-13).

These covenants reiterate the same promise and commission God gave to Adam and Eve. Why would God still want His earth filled with people when He knew they were sinful and enslaved to the enemy? It can only be because He knew that, through the blood of Christ, He would be able to call out a people for Himself from among the nations of the earth to follow Christ's— the Last Adam's—commission to live in intimacy with God and subdue the earth.

These testimonies demonstrate that the Fall of Man *failed* to diminish God's interest in having an earth filled with people who live in relationship with Him, people among whom He dwells and *walks,* as He walked with Adam in the Garden. These testimonies tell us that God's nature and His purposes for mankind have not changed! After all, history is *His story.*

God is making His people to "be fruitful and multiply," but He is doing it through the new birth in His Spirit, creating, as John 1:12-13 puts it, "children of

God…who were born, not of blood, nor of the will of the flesh, nor of the will of man, but of God."

He still intends to establish His Kingdom on the earth by co-laboring with His children. He could easily take dominion of the earth in a moment, but His glory and love are most fully expressed when His rule is extended through His covenant relationship with those He made in His image, who worship Him by choice.

Our Destiny—From Glory to Glory

If the Cross made it possible for us to have the same relationship with God that Christ had and bear the same fruit, then why don't we see a glorious Church ruling and reigning with Christ already? I believe it has to do in part with how the Church has failed to use her inheritance, the testimony, to release His power into the earth.

When there is a failure to "keep the testimony," the revelation of the nature and will of God cannot be sustained from generation to generation. Revivals have come along periodically when, as in the reign of Josiah, the testimony has been found again and has called believers back to the truth of God's nature and their calling.

But since the first century, I am not aware of any generation that burned with the conviction that the testimony of God's activities among men from the past has been their inheritance to equip them for the present. And not just for the purpose of receiving encouragement from the experiences of others, but also to fully apprehend the experience and fruitfulness from what is provided through such an inheritance and pass it on to the next generation. Therefore, these moves of God have not been sustained beyond a single generation.

In response to this, some people have proposed a version of history based on the failure of humanity rather than the nature of God. Many seminarians and historians are taught that Christian revivals typically last two to six years. Revivals, this view suggests, occur mainly to give the Church a shot in the arm, after which everyone should expect business as usual to resume.

Historically this is accurate. But the conclusion that this is the purpose for revival is inaccurate. The will of God then becomes defined through what the Church has done instead of what God has made available.

This interpretation of history is absolutely wrong in that it is based on false definitions of the nature of revival and ultimately of the nature of God. God is abundantly good all the time, and His covenant of love endures forever. Because of these qualities He has purposed in His heart to fill His earth with people made in His image walking in right relationship with Him and exercising their delegated authority over the earth. That is what His Kingdom looks like. It's established in Heaven, and it is being established on earth through the co-laboring of His Church and His Spirit.

Isaiah prophesied that the Kingdom is continually advancing: "Of the increase of His government and peace there will be no end, upon the throne of David and over His kingdom, to order it and establish it with judgment and justice from that time forward, even forever" (Isa. 9:7).

When Christ ascended, He sat down on the throne of David. On the Day of Pentecost, the Father sent the promised Holy Spirit to empower the disciples to establish the Kingdom on earth and fulfill Christ's commission to make disciples of all nations.

What most people miss about the Day of Pentecost is that the harvest of 3,000 converts was not simply the fruit of Peter's preaching. Certainly the Gospel was declared with boldness, but people heard it and were convicted because there had been a shift in the spiritual atmosphere caused by the outpouring of the Spirit.

In other words, when believers allow the Holy Spirit to have His way, the atmosphere is transformed, making it easier for people to come to God. Such a change in mind-set doesn't just happen. It is the impact of the presence of God doing as He pleases with His people. The co-laboring role brings exponential increase to the impact of the Holy Spirit's activities among men. Second Corinthians 4:3-4 explains that the spiritual atmosphere affects people's ability to receive the Gospel:

> *But even if our gospel is veiled, it is veiled to those who are perishing, whose minds the god of this age has blinded, who do not believe, lest the light of the gospel of the glory of Christ, who is the image of God, should shine on them.*

At Pentecost, the "god of the age" was bound, and the light of Christ pierced through the spiritual darkness over Jerusalem, where the crowds had crucified Him weeks earlier. It was as though the wind of God that filled the upper room made a distinct sound as it blew across the hearts of yielded people.

The sound drew people. It was a roar, a sound from Heaven that arrested the hearts of a people who had previously celebrated His death. They were now asking what they must do to be saved. The sound from Heaven released the atmosphere of Heaven until the prevailing powers of darkness gave way to the superiority of light.

That is the normal Christian life. Anything less is going backward. This spiritual shift is precisely what happens in true revival. In revival, the outpouring of the Holy Spirit brings an invasion of the presence of the King of Heaven, which displaces the prince of darkness. The result of this displacement is that people experience the life and power of the Kingdom. Bodies are healed, souls are delivered and saved, believers grow in unity, and ultimately, society and the earth are transformed.

True revival not only calls people to pursue God, but also to pursue their purpose in history and to partner with Him in establishing His dominion over all things. The Holy Spirit doesn't come to give us a shot in the arm; He comes to help us run the race to the end and pass the baton to the next generation with the intent that Kingdom momentum will increase with each succeeding generation.

True revival is an outpouring of the Spirit that brings the Kingdom until there is transformation unto reformation. The nature of the Kingdom is continual advancement. It follows, then, that revival is meant to be sustained throughout the generations, until "the knowledge of the glory of God" covers the earth "as the waters cover the sea" (Hab. 2:14).

Redefining the nature of God and the nature of revival is simply not an option for the Body of Christ in answering the question of why the Church has not stepped into her destiny. The problem is never on His side of the equation; it is always on ours.

We have not renewed our thinking by defining ourselves according to His truth; thus, we live with limitations that He has not given for us. You and I have the chance in our generation to repent from seeing history through a finite perspective and to increase our experience of the transforming power of the testimonies of God, our inheritance. These have been given to the Church to sustain the move of His Spirit among His people and take us from "glory to glory" (2 Cor. 3:18).

Our family history in God is one of the primary things that God has established to train us up to walk in our destiny in this hour. If we will embrace the challenge to study, teach, and experience it, we will enable this generation to step into their identity and purpose as the children of God.

CHAPTER 3

Encountering
His Mercy

The testimony of Scripture is essential in training the people of God to fully engage their divine purpose. These stories may have even played a role in training Jesus to fulfill His destiny. Even though Jesus is the Word (God), He no doubt studied the Scriptures, as He is also fully man. He knew first hand that God is bigger than His Book—as the Book itself testifies. God has hidden the mysteries of His Kingdom in its pages, but only a heart hungry for intimacy with Him will be granted access to unlock those mysteries.

This is much different than merely knowing about Him. Thus, many read the Bible, but not all follow in the footsteps of Christ and enter into the *life* to which it points. We must recognize that it is our *response* to the Scriptures that reveals whether we have truly understood both what God has said and His purposes in saying it.

In John 5, Jesus rebuked the Pharisees for their wrong response to the Scriptures in a statement in which He also addressed the matter of the testimony concerning His identity as the Messiah:

If I bear witness of Myself, My witness is not true. There is another who bears witness of Me, and I know that the witness which He witnesses of Me is true. You have sent to John, and he has borne witness to the truth. Yet I do not receive testimony from man, but I say these things that you may be saved. He was the burning and shining lamp, and you were willing for a time to rejoice in his light. But I have a greater witness than John's; for the works which the Father has given Me to finish—the very works that I do— bear witness of Me, that the Father has sent Me. And the Father Himself, who sent Me, has testified of Me. You have neither heard His voice at any time, nor seen His form. But you do not have His word abiding in you, because whom He sent, Him you do not believe. You search the Scriptures, for in them you think you have eternal life; and these are they which testify of Me. But you are not willing to come to Me that you may have life (John 5:31-40).

Consider first Jesus' discourse concerning the witnesses of who He is. He is unmistakably appealing here to a key principle of the testimony reiterated throughout Scripture: "By the mouth of two or three witnesses shall every word be established" (2 Cor. 13:1).

Jesus is arguing that His *greater* witness consists of two things—His miraculous works and the testimony of His Father revealed through the Scriptures. Later, Jesus declared, "The Father who dwells in Me does the works" (John 14:10), which confirms the implication in this passage, that the Father is the One who provided both of these witnesses that work in tandem to establish the matter of Jesus' identity as the Messiah. This is a clear example of how God intends the Scriptures to work in tandem *with* His works in revealing who He is. We need both in order to know Him.

Jesus' words also point out something fundamental about what happens when God gives a testimony, something that shows *how* the witness of God is greater than any human witness.

God's Word and His works cannot be separated. Everything in existence came to be because He spoke it into being. One of the primary reasons He is called *holy* is that His words have such perfect integrity with His Person that they release the force and reality of His being to accomplish the things He has said.

SCRIPTURE LEADS TO ENCOUNTER

Because of the nature of His Word, God's primary purpose in delivering the Scriptures to us, as Jesus points out in this passage, is to train us *to anticipate and recognize Him when He reveals Himself through His divine acts.*

Jesus said that the evidence that the Pharisees did not have the Word abiding in them was the fact that they didn't believe Jesus and come to Him to receive life. The implication is that the primary purpose of the abiding Word is to prepare and position us for divine encounters that we might respond with faith. Faith is the primary evidence of the Word abiding in us.

It is sobering to realize that if we have unbelief in our hearts, we can read the Scriptures, but we will fail to hear the voice of the Father giving testimony to who He is in its verses. Unbelief literally blinds and deafens our hearts to His voice, thereby effectively blocking the most powerful thing in the universe from being active in and through us.

If we fail to hear His voice, we cannot help but fail to respond to God in the way He desires, with faith that reaches out to *know by experience* the God revealed in the testimony. This is what the example of the Pharisees proves. Without faith that gives us an understanding of how God's testimony works, we will miss Him when He shows up right in front of us!

This issue of how we respond to the Scriptures is present whenever we read them. The entire testimony of Scripture resonates with this theme: *God reveals Himself to mankind, and we either respond with faith or with unbe-*

lief, creating conditions that affect the way God will relate to us.

We are going to see how this truth permeates what the Bible has to say concerning the testimony as we now turn our attention to the portions of Scripture in which the word *testimony* is first introduced.

THE ARK THAT CARRIED THE TESTIMONY

In doing a word study of the word *testimony* in the Bible, it is noteworthy that the first time the word appears, in Exodus 16:34, it refers not merely to a testimony, but *the* Testimony.

The second time the word appears is within the phrase "the Ark of the Testimony." (See Exod. 25:16.) After just two references, then, it is clear that we need to go back and review the highlights of the Exodus story so we can get the context for how the Testimony and the Ark of the Testimony came into being.

The story of how God delivered the people of Israel from Egypt is undoubtedly one of the most dramatic and miraculous in all of human history. God pulled out all the stops in His deliverance of Israel—first devastating the Egyptians with ten plagues, then parting the Red Sea, and then providing the entire group in the desert with miraculously sweetened water and mysterious bread from Heaven.

All of these displays were leading up to something, however. When the people reached Mount Sinai, God made the people an offer:

You have seen what I did to the Egyptians, and how I bore you on eagles' wings and brought you to Myself. Now therefore, if you will indeed obey My voice and keep My covenant, then you shall be a special treasure to Me above all people; for all the earth is Mine. And you shall be to Me a kingdom of priests and a holy nation... (Exodus 19:4-6).

After the people agreed to this offer, God spelled out the initial details of this covenant to Moses, starting with the Ten Commandments. Moses read these to the people, and they said they would obey them. And then God met with Moses for forty days on Mount Sinai and spent the entire time detailing how to build His house and how to carry out the ministry within it. Significantly, God spent twice as much time talking about where He was going to dwell among the people and how they were to approach Him as He did talking about the rules He wanted them to live by. We'll consider this more in a moment.

It is also significant that the Ark was the first item that God detailed to Moses in His blueprints for the Tabernacle. The Ark was to be the central piece of furniture in God's house, for a reason that the following passage makes clear:

They shall make an ark of acacia wood; two and a half cubits shall be its length, a cubit and a half its width, and a cubit and a half its height. And you shall overlay it with pure gold, inside and out you shall overlay it, and shall make a molding of gold all around. You shall cast four rings of gold for it and put them in its four corners; two rings shall be on one side, and two rings on the other side. And you shall make poles of acacia wood, and overlay them with gold. You shall put the poles into the rings on the sides of the ark, that the ark may be carried by them. The poles shall be in the rings of the ark; they shall not be taken from it. And you shall put into the ark the Testimony which I will give you. You shall make a mercy seat of pure gold; two and a half cubits shall be its length and a cubit and a half its width. And you shall make two cherubim of gold; of hammered work you shall make them at the two ends of the mercy seat. Make one cherub at one end, and the other cherub at the other end; you shall make the cherubim at the two ends of it of one piece with the mercy seat. And the cherubim shall stretch out their wings above, covering the mercy seat with their wings, and they shall face one another; the faces of the cherubim shall be toward the mercy seat. You shall put the mercy seat on top of the ark, and in the ark you shall put the Testimony that I will give you. And there I will meet with you, and I will speak with you from above the mercy seat, from between the two cherubim which are on the ark of the Testimony, about everything which I will give you in commandment to the children of Israel (Exodus 25:10-22).

The Ark was the holiest item in the Tabernacle because it was upon this piece of furniture that the cloud of God's presence specifically rested. It was called the Ark of the Testimony because, as you just read, the Testimony lived inside of this box upon which God sat.

Eventually we see what the Testimony is in the concluding verse of Moses' encounter with God: "And when He had made an end of speaking with him on Mount Sinai, He gave Moses two tablets of the Testimony, tablets of stone, written with the finger of God" (Exod.31:18). (The tablets actually placed in the Ark were the copies Moses made after he broke the originals in anger over the Israelites' sin.) However, two more testimony items were eventually kept in the Ark of the Testimony along with these stone tablets. The writer of Hebrews describes the contents of the Ark succinctly:

...behind the second veil, the part of the tabernacle which is called the Holiest of All, which had the golden censer and the ark of the covenant overlaid on all sides with gold, in which were the golden pot that had the manna, Aaron's rod that budded, and the tablets of the covenant; and above it were the cherubim of glory overshadowing the mercy seat... (Hebrews 9:3-5).

Before we look at the significance of these items, notice that after Moses placed these items in the Ark, they were not taken out. The people never saw them again.

Obviously, God didn't command this to keep the people in ignorance of the commands written on the stone tablets, as He had Moses write down everything in the Book of the Law to teach the people. So the question is, why would God insist that the people of Israel carry this tent with all of these items around in the desert when they had the Book that told them everything that God wanted them to do? After all, that was all the Israelites themselves were interested in having, as they had become frightened of His presence. As the proceedings at the mountain continued, God displayed His power so strongly with thunder, lightning, and other signs that they insisted Moses speak to God on their behalf. But while God allowed Moses to be a mediator between Him and the people, He was not content merely to give them the rules for how to live and then sit back to enforce them. God's people were not to be known for the perfect law code they possessed, but by the fact that God Himself was present among them.

This is the reason God spent more time telling them how to build His house than He did telling them how He expected them to behave. Everything in this house had a symbolic, prophetic dimension that revealed an aspect of the nature of God and His relationship with the people.

Everything that was done in this house was focused on stewarding that relationship through approaching God in prayer and worship. And just to make sure that they didn't confuse His house with Him, He had them follow His cloud in the desert for years and set up the Tabernacle wherever He stopped. Many times the people would see "Him" visiting Moses at the Tent of Meeting. More than His house or His laws, it was His presence that gave them their identity, purpose, and self-definition.

For this reason, we must put it into our minds that the Testimony was not merely words on a page or stone tablet, nor a collection of holy relics. The words that were written were only significant because of the One who said them, and He insisted that along with those words, the people keep tangible evidence that He was able to fulfill what He had promised.

Each element of the Testimony kept in the Ark was a physical reality that embodied a revelation God had given to His people through specific, miraculous acts. The stone tablets expressed His encounter with them on Mount Sinai. They memorialized the fact that the covenant was made between a living God and His people, and that His commands outlined how they were to relate to Him and one another.

The jar of manna embodied the revelation of His supernatural provision for them. Interestingly, this provision was not just for their bodies, but also for their souls, because in giving them the manna God also pre-scribed the Sabbath day of rest and recreation and pro-vided enough manna on the sixth day so they wouldn't have to work at gathering any for the seventh day of the week.

The rod of Aaron represents the revelation of God's mark of delegated authority among the people. At one point the people questioned the authority of Aaron, so they put twelve dead almond branches from the leaders of the twelve tribes in the Tabernacle overnight. When they retrieved them the next day, Aaron's rod had mirac-ulously sprouted, budded, blossomed, and borne ripe almonds (Num. 17:8). This revealed that God's appointed leadership must always be identified by the manifestation of resurrection life. For in the same way that Aaron's dead almond rod had new life as seen in *sprouts, buds, blossoms, and ripe almonds,* so it is essential that leaders be growing in all areas of life. It is noteworthy that there is life, but not necessarily maturity (ripe almonds) in every area.

TESTIMONIES REVEAL COVENANT

As we saw in the above passage, the mercy seat that rested over these items of testimony was the place where God would abide. We must not miss the significance of this—His mercy rests upon the testimony. This makes sense when we consider that *the Testimony* was used inter-changeably with *the Covenant.*

The whole focus of a covenant is upon the relationship between the parties that have entered into it. Obviously, without guidelines for the relationship upon which these parties agree, there can be no relationship. The Testimony performed the vital task of describing the nature of the covenantal relationship (that God entered into with His people, and they with Him) and defining the context in which it was to be walked out.

But the guidelines He gave them were only meaningful because He intended to have an actual relationship with them. It would strike us as absurd to think of getting married, only to act like the thing our spouse most wanted was for us to study our vows on a daily basis and try to go about doing what we said we would do, with no personal contact. This would not lead to a successful marriage.

Unfortunately, the response I have just described, along with a host of other responses that result from the ignorance and unbelief that man inherited from the Fall, characterized this generation of Israelites and has characterized generations of mankind throughout history.

Thus, this Testimony and Old Covenant reflect God's full awareness of Israel's sinful condition. God had to put up some strong boundaries so that sinful man could approach Him without dying instantly. Those boundaries were not to keep people away, but to teach them what God requires of those who stand before Him.

When the Israelites finally reached Mount Sinai, they had already exhibited less than exemplary behavior, from complaining about the water and food and begging to go back to Egypt to gathering extra manna when they weren't supposed to and then going out to gather it on the Sabbath when there was none.

God knew that these former slaves were far from understanding how to approach Him, so He set up strict parameters for their first few meetings. He told them to consecrate themselves and stay away from the mountain, "lest He break out against them" (Exod. 19:24). This is the point where He started up the fireworks, and the people got it right—God is absolutely holy and awesome. The people were frightened, but they missed what Moses understood, which was *why* God was displaying His power and holiness:

> *Now all the people witnessed the thunderings, the lightning flashes, the sound of the trumpet, and the mountain smoking; and when the people saw it, they trembled and stood afar off. Then they said to Moses, "You speak with us, and we will hear; but let not God speak with us, lest we die." And Moses said to the people, "Do not fear; for God has come to test you, and that His fear may be before you, so that you may not sin." So the people stood afar off, but Moses drew near the thick darkness where God was* (Exodus 20:18-21).

The people thought they needed to move away from God rather than learn how to approach Him, as Moses did. This choice, along with other choices the people made, such as the decision to worship a golden calf only a few days after making covenant with God, led God to establish a worship ritual that was entirely carried out by the priests on behalf of the people. Remember, originally He offered to make Israel a kingdom of priests. What they ended up with was a tribe of priests, and only the High Priest was allowed before the Ark once a year on the Day of Atonement.

In His mercy, God hid Himself from those who, because their hearts were hard, would be destroyed by standing in a place of unhindered access to His manifest glory. He didn't reject them because they had rejected Him. He simply made provision, in the way the Tabernacle was set up and through sacrifices (particularly the lamb sacrificed for sin on the Day of Atonement), for His own just nature to be honored, at least provisionally, so that He was able to remain among them.

These guidelines to protect people from His holiness were for everyone. But both Moses and David had become so set apart to God that He seemed to give them exemption from the Law that they might come closer into His presence.

Earlier I stated that our response of either faith or unbelief to God's revelation creates conditions that affect the way God relates to us. This is clearly portrayed in the history surrounding the Testimony. This means that

God's will has various measures, or dimensions in different circumstances according to these conditions.

The Bible is confusing and contradictory if you think that everything God says and does is an expression of His highest will. For example, in the Old Testament we read, "The soul who sins shall die" (Ezek. 18:4). In the New Testament we read, "The Lord is not slack concerning His promise, as some count slackness, but is longsuffering toward us, not willing that any should perish but that all should come to repentance" (2 Pet. 3:9). This second expression of the will of God is higher than the first, and God revealed it when the conditions of His relationship with us changed because of what Christ accomplished on the Cross.

A MAN AFTER GOD'S HEART

But even before Christ came, there was someone who followed in Moses' footsteps and chose to "[draw] near the thick darkness where God was."

David was a unique individual in the Old Testament because he discovered the hidden dimensions of God's higher will for His relationship with His people. He discovered that God didn't really want the blood of bulls and goats but the sacrifice of a contrite and thankful heart.

This discovery led him to do something unimaginable. He took the Ark of the Covenant, the Ark that only the High Priest was allowed to see once a year, and brought it into a tabernacle of His own design, where he had priests worshiping around it 24 hours a day for years. He didn't do this casually, especially after a man died in the initial attempt to bring the Ark to Jerusalem on a cart. But his heart for the presence of God led him to establish a personal, passionate expression of worship before the Ark that, technically, should have been illegal for a man who was not a priest, or even for anyone who lived before the blood of Jesus was shed.

The Psalmist said, "Your testimonies also are my delight and my counselors," and "I have more under-standing than all my teachers, for Your testimonies are my meditation" (Ps. 119:24,99). Wisdom, insight, and passion for God are gained through testimonies.

It is also probable that David's heart for God was expressed in a continual study of the Testimony (see Ps. 139:8,14, and Ps. 145:4,5,9) that unlocked the revelation of its nature as a context for meeting with God (the mercy seat) and as a guide for approaching God. As a result, God permitted him to come into His presence and experience a measure of the communion and worship that would become available to every New Testament believer. This, along with the fact that God named David as the ancestor of His Son, the Messiah, reveals that David understood what the Testimony was all about.

After all, the question raised by the whole history of God delivering the Testimony to Israel is, *Why would God want to establish a covenant with sinful people?* Why would He want a system of worship that failed to solve the sin issue, especially since He already knew how He was going to deal with that issue through the Cross?

I've hinted at it, and we've already seen the answer to these questions in Jesus' rebuke to the Pharisees. God gave the Testimony to train and prepare His people for the coming of the Messiah. Galatians 3:24 explains: "The law was our tutor to bring us to Christ, that we may be justified by faith." David saw that the Testimony and Old Covenant did not reflect God's highest desire, and thus that they were designed to prepare the people to cry out for and recognize the Messiah.

JESUS: THE LIVING TESTIMONY

Jesus declared that He came to fulfill the Law and the prophets (see Matt. 5:17), or in other words, the requirements of the Old Covenant. This fulfillment has many rich dimensions to it, which the New Testament writers and many others have explored.

In particular, the Book of Hebrews acts as a bookend for the Exodus account of the giving of the Testimony and the building of the Tabernacle by detailing how each aspect of the Tabernacle's furniture and the ministry within it prophesied the superior, spiritual ministry accomplished by Christ through His death and resurrection.

Hebrews describes Jesus as our High Priest who represented man to God and God to man. In representing us to God, He entered the actual, spiritual Holy of Holies in Heaven and presented His own blood at the mercy seat to atone for our sins (see Heb. 9:11-12). But in representing God to man, Christ was the Tabernacle of God among men, as John 1:14 says, "The Word became flesh and dwelt [tabernacled] among us."

Thus, Jesus embodied the realities to which the Ark of the Testimony pointed. The box of acacia wood (the same material Noah used to build his ark) spoke of the redemption Jesus offered to the world. The gold spoke of the glory of God that rested in and upon Him. The cherubim spoke of the angelic presence that surrounded Him. The mercy seat, where the blood of the lamb was smeared and where God met with Moses, spoke of the unhindered access and forgiveness that Jesus extended to mankind from the Father. And finally, Jesus embodied the elements of the Testimony within the Ark—the tablets, the manna, and the rod of Aaron—by perfectly fulfilling the Law, by creating miraculous provision, and by walking in the anointing and authority of Heaven, evidenced by the release of resurrection life.

Christ was the living Testimony of God to the world. Everything He was, said, and did revealed the nature of the covenant that God desired to have all along with His sons and daughters. With His life and in His death He created the *context* for us to approach God, know Him and walk with Him.

Being "in Christ" means that we actually get to participate in both dimensions of Christ's priestly ministry. In Christ we also minister to God with spiritual worship in the Holy of Holies, which we enter through the "new and living way" Christ Himself has made for us:

> *Therefore, brethren, having boldness to enter the Holiest by the blood of Jesus, by a new and living way which He consecrated for us, through the veil, that is, His flesh, and having a High Priest over the house of God, let us draw near with a true heart in full assurance of faith, having our hearts sprinkled from an evil conscience and our bodies washed with pure water* (Hebrews 10:19-22).

And on the other hand, being in Christ means that we experience the indwelling of the Holy Spirit. Thus, the Holy of Holies now resides in us. Paul asked, "Do you not know that you are the temple of God and that the Spirit of God dwells in you?" (1 Cor. 3:16). This means that we are now carriers of the Testimony—carriers of the realities of God's New Covenant with man through His Son, as He declared through the prophet Jeremiah:

> *Behold, the days are coming, says the Lord, when I will make a new covenant with the house of Israel and with the house of Judah—not according to the covenant that I made with their fathers in the day that I took them by the hand to lead them out of the land of Egypt, My covenant which they broke, though I was a husband to them, says the Lord. But this is the covenant that I will make with the house of Israel after those days, says the Lord: I will put My law in their minds, and write it on their hearts; and I will be their God, and they shall be My people. No more shall every man teach his neighbor, and every man his brother, saying, "Know the*

Lord," for they all shall know Me, from the least of them to the greatest of them... (Jeremiah 31:31-34).

Our job is to learn how to release the reality and power of the Testimony in the same way Jesus did. Jesus represented God much differently than the Ark of the Testimony represented Him. There is a significant difference between a box of inanimate objects that points to spiritual realities and a living testimony that interacts with and manifests those realities.

While the box could only preserve the relics of what God had done, Jesus declared and demonstrated the works of God for all to see. He revealed the secret of His ministry liberally to His disciples by reiterating often that He did only what He saw His Father doing and said only what He heard His Father say. That is, He and His Father were exactly alike, were in perfect agreement.

Likeness and agreement are the heart of covenant. It was this perfect agreement with God that enabled Jesus to release the Spirit of God whenever He spoke. In His words and works, He literally *re-presented* the God of the Testimony. As we saw in the previous chapter, Christ has given us access to this superior covenant relationship with God and called us to represent Him in the same way. Thus, keeping the testimony is not a matter of preserving what God has done in our memories, but of revealing what God is like to those around us through declaration and demonstration.

The very word *testimony* in Hebrew comes from a root word that means "to repeat, to do again." Notice that this repetition carries within it the two dimensions of *saying* and *doing*. The testimony is something to be repeated, both in word and in deed. This derives directly from the nature of the Word of God that we looked at earlier. His words cannot be separated from His works.

It also derives from His nature as a covenant-making and covenant-keeping God. When we declare the testimonies of the Lord, we are actually describing *who* He has promised to be in relationship with us; and more, we are putting a demand on Heaven for that covenant to be renewed and demonstrated in the present as it was in the past.

And as we'll see later, putting this demand on Heaven is exactly what God wants us to do. He commands us to repeat His testimonies, because in doing so we create an atmosphere and an opportunity for Him to do again what He has done. Just as Jesus did, we are to create a context for His presence within us to be released to those around us through the declaration of the testimony.

We carry the mercy seat of Christ wherever we go. When we declare the testimonies of God to people, we are setting them up to *meet* God in the same way we are declaring. This is a powerful reality, but one that we only anticipate and access consistently when we learn to follow in the footsteps of David and make the testimonies of the Lord our delight and our counselors. If we are going to fulfill our role in this covenant relationship, we must learn to *keep* the testimony, and in doing so learn to release His power to the world around us.

CHAPTER 4

Keeping the Testimony

Deuteronomy is the book that every devout Jew had to learn backward and forward growing up, for a simple reason: it is one of the most practical books in the Bible. It has practical instructions for just about every aspect of community life, relationships, family, work, and worship. And because it was so vital to Israel's success as God's covenant people, one of the first practical instructions in the book is *how to learn what it says*:

> *And these words which I command you today shall be in your heart. You shall teach them diligently to your children, and shall talk of them when you sit in your house, when you walk by the way, when you lie down, and when you rise up. You shall bind them as a sign on your hand, and they shall be as frontlets between your eyes. You shall write them on the doorposts of your house and on your gates* (Deuteronomy 6:6-9).

In summary, God wanted His people to do three basic things with Deuteronomy. It was to be the primary subject of their children's education. It was also to be the main topic in their conversation throughout the day as they were to surround themselves with visible reminders of what it said. These three disciplines were keys for successfully *keeping* the three primary dimensions of the words God had spoken to them. "You shall diligently keep the *commandments* of the Lord your God, His *testimonies,* and His *statutes,* which He has commanded you" (Deut. 6:17).

Keeping the commandments of the Lord is fairly easy to understand. It simply means to do what they say. If He says to honor your parents, you honor your parents. Keeping the statutes of the Lord is slightly different. God's statutes are the principles and supreme values underlying His commandments and regulations for our lives. For example, He promises that we will possess long life by fulfilling the command to honor our parents. This reveals a statute of His nature and Kingdom—that life flows through honor. God commands us to keep His statutes because He does not want us only to do what He says; He wants us to understand why He commands us to do certain things. He wants us to understand the principles that govern His world so that we can mature as sons and daughters who think like Him and live successfully by ordering our lives His way.

But what does it mean to keep the testimonies of the Lord? To answer this question, we need to go back and look at the significance of the disciplines prescribed in

Deuteronomy 6:6-9. These verses indicate that along with the commandments and statutes, we are to tell the testimonies, the stories of God's supernatural interventions in history, to our children, we are to keep them in our daily conversations, and we are to build memorials to remind us of them. In short, we are continually to *remember* and *declare* them.

The word *keep* means to "watch" or "preserve." The idea is clear—keep your eyes focused on what God has done, the testimony, and protect it from obscurity. I like to think of the testimony of Jesus as *the lens through which I see life.* A supernatural history is easy for people to forget, especially when they want to feel good about themselves in the absence of miracles. When miracles are absent, and we are followers of Jesus, we instinctively want to create a reason why they are missing so we can live in our present state without making radical changes. It is too easy to create theological reasons for the absence of miracles. Instead we are to find out why they are missing and pursue the One who requires the supernatural from us.

POWER-FILLED DECLARATION

The testimony of the Lord must be declared, as there is a clear connection between declaration and the release of power.

Beginning in Genesis 1, the Bible sets us up to understand that nothing happens in the Kingdom unless first there is a declaration. And this is true whether God

Releasing the Spirit of Prophecy

speaks directly or whether He puts His words in the mouths of His people.

God's original commission to Adam to help define the nature of the world he was to live in by naming the animals speaks of the power of declaration that He vested in mankind from the beginning. After the Fall, there were only a handful of people who responded to God's call to be His prophets. But many of these individuals tapped into God's heart and purpose to restore His people to a place of purity and intimacy where everyone, not just a few, could hear what God was saying and declare it, releasing the reality of what was declared into the world around them. Moses said, "Oh that all the Lord's people were prophets and that the Lord would put His Spirit upon them!" (Num. 11:29).

Joel declared, "And it shall come to pass afterward that I will pour out My Spirit on all flesh; your sons and your daughters shall prophesy, your old men shall dream dreams, your young men shall see visions" (Joel 2:28). And Isaiah described the reason that God wanted everyone to have access to the prophetic anointing when God spoke through Isaiah saying, "I have put My words in your mouth; I have covered you with the shadow of My hand, that I may plant the heavens, lay the foundations of the earth, and say to Zion, 'You are My people'" (Isa. 51:16).

Where are the heavens to be planted? In the same place God has laid foundations—on the earth. This

≈ 78 ≈

idea of "planting the heavens" is echoed in the declaration Jesus taught us: "Your kingdom come. Your will be done on earth as it is in heaven" (Matt. 6:10). This is a prophetic declaration that is not so much focused on foretelling a future event but on calling something into existence.

Jesus modeled both of these aspects of the prophetic ministry for us. He not only foretold events, but His words actually caused things to happen the moment they left His mouth. The way He put it was, "The words I speak to you are spirit and they are life" (John 6:63). When He spoke, He released the Spirit of God into the atmosphere, and the superior reality of the Kingdom of God, which is in the Spirit, began to transform earthly reality.

It is vital to remember that Jesus did everything in His earthly ministry as a man who had set aside all His divine privileges and power in order to model the Christian life for us. He demonstrated that we also, by speaking with the presence and power of the Holy Spirit, would release the Holy Spirit to "plant the heavens," transforming the world around us.

A true prophetic word changes the atmosphere and acts as a catalyst that sets a chain of events in motion to bring the word to pass. This is why Paul exhorted us to "pursue love, and desire spiritual gifts, but especially that you may prophesy" (1 Cor. 14:1). We should all be possessed with a desire, not necessarily to hold the office of a prophet, but to grow in the grace of the Spirit to hear and declare what God is saying. That is what opens the heavens and attracts the angelic realm into our circumstances, because angels' primary job is to enforce and establish the Word of God when it's declared.

This truth is the driving principle behind the priority of declaring the testimony. Remember, as we saw in the first chapter, "The testimony of Jesus is the spirit of prophecy" (Rev. 19:10). When we declare the works of God, we release a creative, prophetic anointing that changes the atmosphere. In fact, *the declared testimony creates access for the very anointing that brought about the testimony in the first place—which was also released through a declaration—to bring it about again.*

This is the reality embedded in the very word *testimony*—"to do again." I've seen this happen too many times to doubt that when we declare the testimony of the Lord, God releases His authority to enforce the word and duplicate the miracle.

Declaring the testimony doesn't need to look like preaching. Declarations can simply be speaking words out loud. For this reason, Deuteronomy says the testimony is supposed to be in our *conversations*. Once, I was talking with a man and he happened to mention that he had a lump on his collarbone. He explained that it had never healed properly when he'd broken it several years earlier. I responded by saying that I saw broken bones healed all the time. His wife grabbed his hand, put it on the lump, and said, "You're healed!" Just like that, the bone was perfectly smooth. It was the power of the testimony.

This same dynamic explains why I've found that one of the fastest ways to initiate people into a life of miracles is to have them go to Brazil on a "Global Awakening" trip with Randy Clark. On any one of these trips you can potentially witness thousands of miracles taking place. And these miracles take place through the average, everyday Christian who left the sometimes "oppressive" environment of the North American Church to be used in a country that has no problem with the God of miracles.

What happens after the meetings is significant: when the teams are sitting at dinner or hanging out, they talk about the miracles. They don't want to talk about the issues back home—the bills that are due or the denominational conflicts they're dealing with. They want to talk about the fact that they just watched someone with no pupils in her eyes suddenly develop them and gain her sight, or the tumors that disappeared, or the quadriplegic that got out of his wheelchair and walked.

By the time they get home, these conversations have built a momentum in their lives that brings them into realms of power they never knew they could experience in their own lives. They've been jump-started into a lifestyle of ongoing miracles by declaring the testimony.

Now, I need to point out that as I have traveled and ministered over the last many years, I have found that this understanding of the prophetic nature of the testimony comes as news for many people.

In most places, people have a value for the testimony, just as I myself did growing up. I loved to hear people's stories of how God had encountered them and changed their lives forever. It was always encouraging and led me to give praise and honor to God. But I don't remember a single instance when the specific miracle that had been declared in those testimonies was instantly duplicated among those who heard them. I'm not saying it didn't happen, but I was never aware of it (beyond someone responding to an altar call to receive Christ after someone's testimony of conversion.)

The truth is that the anointing on the testimony has always been there, but our ignorance has kept us from receiving what we never perceived as available. As Scripture says, "My people are destroyed for lack of knowledge" (Hos. 4:6). Without revelation of how God works, we can't reach out with faith and grab hold of the heavenly potential that is in the atmosphere around us. This is what we see in the story of the woman with the issue of blood (see Mark 5). Jesus was being touched and pressed in on all sides by a crowd of people. But only one person saw that she could actually receive something simply by touching Him. She had a revelation of what was available, and therefore had faith to reach out and grab hold of it.

Stewardship Through Meditation

Stewardship begins with understanding what we have been given and why.

We have much to be thankful for in this hour. The Holy Spirit is restoring the revelation of the power of the testimony to release miracles to His people and which is available to all of us. It's within reach. God is mercifully bringing us out of our ignorance, from faith to faith and from glory to glory.

But I also want to emphasize another truth about the Kingdom. In response to His disciples' conversation about whether the Kingdom was going to appear on the earth suddenly, Jesus told them a parable about a man who entrusted his servants with a certain amount of money to steward. Based on their faithfulness with the money, the servants were eventually entrusted with measures of authority over cities (see Luke 19:11-27). The parable of the minas teaches us that when God unlocks the wealth of His kingdom for us, He is entrusting us with something we are to steward. It is our *faithful stewardship* that qualifies us to handle the weight of power and authority that rests upon one who can transform the landscape with a declaration.

In unveiling the power of the testimony, God is not just giving us access to a principle of His Kingdom that works. He is really giving us access to the *knowledge of Himself*. Remember, in every story of what God has done, there is an unveiling of His nature and an invitation to know Him experientially in the same way.

That's what the anointing on the testimony is for, because the testimony is part of *covenant*. Its whole purpose is to lead us into relationship with God. But the revelation of God is a weighty thing. When we see who God really is revealed as in His testimonies, we cannot walk away from it without responding to God in one of two ways. Either we allow the revelation of who He is to transform the way we think and perceive reality, or we resist the truth and become hard-hearted. Simply put, either we step toward relationship with God, or we step away from it.

What Deuteronomy teaches us is that if we desire to step toward relationship with God, then we are going to need to be proactive about it. To sit back and merely applaud what God has done actually brings us under a deception wherein we think we have received the revelation in the testimony and responded to God in the way He desires.

We are certainly to give God praise for what He's done, but we can't stop there. Unless the testimony actually transforms the rest of our thinking and behavior, we are not truly *keeping* it. The revelation of God in the testimony is supposed to *train* us to see reality from God's perspective so we can walk in faith. And training of all kinds, whether you're in the military or learning an instrument, requires *practice*. The only way we can truly absorb all the nutrients, so to speak, in the testimony is by making a conscientious decision to develop a lifestyle of talking about God's wondrous works all the time.

Jesus declared, "The violent take [the kingdom] by force" (Matt. 11:12). He also said, "He who is not with me is against Me, and he who does not gather with Me scatters" (Luke 11:23). There is no neutral territory in our world. Either we are forcefully and proactively pursuing the Kingdom of God, or we are, whether actively or passively, allowing the kingdom of darkness to legislate its influence by gaining a place in our hearts—the place from which we perceive reality.

Our hearts are the gates through which the spirit realm interacts with the natural realm, and our thoughts and words open these gates. Jesus described this when He said, "A good man out of the good treasure of his heart brings forth good; and an evil man out of the evil treasure of his heart brings forth evil. For out of the abundance of the heart his mouth speaks" (Luke 6:45).

Our hearts are filled with whatever captures our thoughts and affections. Scripture calls this the *meditation* of our hearts. Notice that meditation in the biblical sense refers to filling the heart and mind, as opposed to Eastern meditation, which tries to empty the mind.

Whatever fills our hearts and minds ultimately leads us to establish some kind of trust or agreement with it. If our thoughts are constantly filled with imagining what bad things could happen to us or those we love, we will establish an agreement with the spirit of anxiety. If we choose to focus on what God isn't doing, it is more likely that we will stumble over questions like, "Why didn't that person get healed?" or "Why is there so much evil in the world?" Then we will establish an agreement with the spirit of bitterness, creating the atmosphere for the spirit of offense to arise, leading us to the ultimate sin of unbelief. But if we fill our minds with what God is doing and what He has done, we build an agreement with the spirit of faith. Whatever we agree with is what will fill our thoughts and mouths, and thus, what we'll release into the world around us.

In fact, the spiritual reality with which we commune in our hearts is precisely the power released in our declarations. For this reason, the words of our mouth and the meditations of our heart are intimately connected. This is why David prayed, "Let the words of my mouth and the meditation of my heart be acceptable in Your sight, O Lord, my strength and my Redeemer" (Ps. 19:14). God exposed the relationship between meditation and declaration to Joshua when He said:

> *This Book of the Law shall not depart from your mouth, but you shall meditate in it day and night, that you may observe to do according to all that is written in it. For then you will make your way prosperous, and then you will have good success* (Joshua 1:8).

The implication of this passage is twofold when it comes to keeping the testimony. First, we are not to declare the testimony as a mindless repetition. We are to engage our minds and imaginations in what we are saying.

Conversely, our meditation on what God has said must involve talking. The Hebrew word for meditation here literally means "to moan, growl, utter, muse, mutter, or speak." This same word was used to describe a lion growling over his prey. Our meditation is not to be a relaxed activity. We are to hunt down and joyfully and ravenously devour the testimony of God. This is how our bodies and minds are trained "to do according to all that is written."

These activities should be obviously practical to us, as we have experienced how learning takes place. The highest levels of learning are consistently accomplished when repetition, physical and mental engagement, critical thinking, and articulation (putting the ideas in our own words) are all present in the learning process.

When we do this with the testimony, there are two primary results. First, when we fill our hearts and minds with the record of what God has done through conversation and meditation, we sustain a constant awareness of the God who invades the impossible. This posture of awareness and expectation creates the hope, faith, courage, and hunger that we need in order to respond to the impossibilities around us.

But the second thing is that, by in effect prophesying over ourselves with the testimony, we release something in the unseen realm that actually draws us into real experiences where we see the impossibilities around us transformed by the God of the testimony. This is what the Lord promised to Joshua—by keeping the testimony, we actually *make our own way* prosperous and successful.

The life of David, one of the most successful men in the Old Testament, and as we have seen, the most profound model of keeping the testimony, certainly speaks of the truth of this promise. All through the Psalms he speaks of declaring the works of God, and proclaims, "The works of the Lord are great, *studied* by all who have pleasure in them" (Ps. 111:2). Psalm 66 gives us a wonderful insight into how David studied and meditated upon the works of God. He says,

> *Come and see the works of God;*
> *He is awesome in His doing toward the sons of men.*
> *He turned the sea into dry land;*
> *They went through the river on foot.*
> *There we will rejoice in Him* (Psalm 66:5-6).

The events to which David is referring here—the miraculous crossings of the Red Sea and the Jordan River—took place hundreds of years before his life. And yet he speaks as if he were inviting us to a party where we would watch these things happen and then celebrate God together.

What David discovered in studying the works of the Lord is that they have a life of their own that is unaffected by time. The God who performed them exists beyond time, and when we study what He has done, we cannot help but stumble upon the fact that these are also the things He is doing and will do.

The Hebrew word translated *study* in this verse also means "to seek after." If we take pleasure in and study the testimonies, we actually *track down* personal encounters with these works of God. It might be better said that we actually pursue these encounters with the works of God as the real "prey" we are hunting down as we *meditate*. And this is exactly what we must do if we are going to experience the fullness of our inheritance in the testimony.

REMEMBERING

Building a lifestyle of declaring the testimony is the first dimension of keeping the testimony. The second dimension is building a lifestyle of *remembering*. These are two sides of the same coin.

I recently discovered something interesting about the Hebrew word for *remember*. It is the root word for the word *male*. This may seem like an obscure correlation, but here it is: The man carries the seed of reproduction. And when you remember God's supernatural interventions in impossible situations, you carry in your heart the seed of yet another miracle.

We've already seen how declaring the testimony creates access to the anointing by which it can be duplicated. Now we see that this is also an act of remembering. When we remember what God has done, it's as though we take the seed of a particular miracle, deposit it in a new environment, and another miracle takes place.

The fact that human beings have the capacity for memory has another side to it, as we all know. We also have an astounding capacity to forget. The consequences of forgetting can be small or great, depending on what is forgotten. The ramifications of forgetting where you put your stapler are much different from forgetting your wedding anniversary.

What is so astounding about our ability to forget is that we are capable of forgetting things that seemed so entirely unforgettable when they happened. On the other hand, we often find that we forget things that didn't seem monumental at the time, but in retrospect were actually terribly important. Both cases reveal our need for some kind of external mechanism that helps us to remember.

When Israel crossed into the Promised Land through the Jordan River, Joshua commanded the elders of the tribes to go back into the river and take out twelve stones from the riverbed and create a pile of them on the bank. Joshua explained the purpose:

...that this may be a sign among you when your children ask in time to come, saying, "What do these stones mean to you?" Then you shall answer them that the waters of the Jordan were cut off before the ark of the covenant of the Lord; when it crossed over the Jordan, the waters of the Jordan were cut off. And these stones shall be for a memorial to the children of Israel forever (Joshua 4:6-7).

The piles of stones were to be *signs* and *memorials,* which are similar in nature. Signs are realities that point to greater realities. Memorials are things that are meant to *remind* you of other things. In this case, these piles of stones reminded the people of the testimony of how God held back the waters of the Jordan and brought His people into the land of promises.

But the supernatural interventions of God in human history are in themselves signs, in that they are realities that point to the greater revelation of God Himself. So the pile of stones was a memorial and a sign that pointed to another sign, which pointed to the reality.

When Johnny and his dad encountered this pile of stones on the river path, he wouldn't only hear the story; he would hear what the story pointed to: "This is what the God of your fathers is like, and He's your God, too!" This was never to be a boring history lesson. Embedded in Israel's culture was the sense that their history as a covenant people contained the promises of whom God would be for each successive generation to come.

We should establish things that jog our memories, things that remind us of what God has done in our lives and who He is. One memorial stone in my life happens to be a classic pre-1964 Winchester rifle that I was given many years ago, when my dad was pastor at Bethel Church and I was on staff under him.

At the time I didn't own a hunting rifle, but I had been saving money for one because I loved to hunt. After I'd saved up enough, I thought it was probably wisest that I pay some bills with the money instead, and did. The next Sunday night I came to church and one of the senior elders came up to me quite unexpectedly and asked, "Bill, do you need a gun?" I said, "Yes, I do." He said, "Come over to my house after church tonight." So I did. I was stunned when he brought out the Winchester, but not only because the gun was very valuable; it was much more than that. It was a pile of stones. It spoke of something bigger than itself, a lesson that God has been teaching me now for years: if I obey in the small things, He rewards in the big things.

Some time later, after we moved to Weaverville, I eventually accumulated four guns, which we kept in a closet (before gun safes were required.) One weekend we left town, and when we came back, somebody had broken into the house and stolen my guns—except for the one that was the most valuable. I don't know why, but I think the Lord may have blinded the thief's eyes to the most valuable gun in the group.

I suppose I could be offended that he or she was able to take the other three guns. But that never crossed my mind. I was so thankful that the thief didn't take the possession that had the most value to me. I needed to have a pile of stones in my life so that I would never forget what He is really like.

Now, what are the eternal consequences of having a rifle? There are none. But it reminds me of the revelation of who He is in my life. I don't hunt with this particular gun anymore, but I'll never get rid of it unless He gives me a word to do so, because it's my pile of stones. It speaks of how God honors wisdom (in my paying my bills) and prophesies of the covenant that I have with God over my life, which is entirely based on His glorious nature.

Memorials are a big deal to God. They don't have to be extravagant. In the Old Testament they were things like piles of stones, words carved on doorways, and colored tassels on articles of clothing. In the New Testament, Jesus gave us the memorial of Communion with bread and wine with which to remember His death and resurrection.

You might also have a journal, a photo album, or a simple object that reminds you of specific times when you encountered God and He revealed Himself. He gave me a gun. It can be anything, but the point is that they should be things you have invested with meaning so that they are signs that point to the testimony—things you see regularly and reflect upon often. Memorials are a key element of keeping the testimony because they work to protect us from our own vulnerability to forget the things that God says are most important. They work like an alarm clock. We don't turn the alarm clock on after we're already out of bed. We set it up in advance so it will trigger a certain reaction from us when the right time comes—usually unexpectedly.

Believers cannot afford to forget their own testimony of conversion. This was one of apostle Paul's secrets in ministry. No matter what was happening in the place he was speaking, he could always revert to his personal story, his testimony. Many religious leaders were in continual conflict with him because they couldn't take away his experience, and his experience was contrary to their view of God.

Whether you've seen thousands of miracles or few, if you've said yes to Jesus, you have a testimony that you must keep close to you. There's a reason that we find God reminding His people throughout the Old Testament that they used to be nobodies and slaves in Egypt and that He saved them and brought them into the Promised Land. He wasn't bragging or rubbing their noses in it. He was reminding them of who they were and how they got there so they could have the right perspective of the present and future.

Your testimony, like all testimonies, is a story about who God is, and what God has done. The New Testament writers spent a good deal of time explaining the meaning of conversion so that we could train our minds to remember according to God's version of the story. However, if we revisit the events of our past with a perspective that is not based on the work of the Cross and the effectiveness of Christ's blood, we are actually opening ourselves up to a spirit of deception.

Scripture tells us that our old man (old nature) died with Christ. The person you and everyone else thought you were doesn't exist anymore. I'm not saying that we don't experience things in our lives that are the results of past choices we made. But their significance has dramatically changed. I once heard a prophetic word where the Lord spoke, saying, "I will not remove the scars from your life. Instead I will arrange them in such a way that they have the appearance of carving on a fine piece of crystal." What once felt hopelessly destructive has become something that reveals the glory and goodness of God.

Regularly and rightly remembering your conversion takes you back to the foundation stone of the Christian life. The truth of all of our stories is that God came to us in our brokenness and weakness and did what we could not do for ourselves. No matter how mature we become in God, the theme of our utter dependence and His perfect ability permanently runs through our lives.

For this reason, when people share testimonies, I encourage them to be really honest about everything that happened, including details of human weakness. For example, if you were very scared about praying for a person with a certain affliction because you didn't believe he or she would get well, tell that. Keep that part of the story intact, because we need to see that the Lord uses the raw act of obedience, and not just great faith.

Conversely, if you knew that you knew that you knew that the person with the terrifying affliction was going to get well, include that in the story, because I also need to see that it is possible to operate in the gift of faith and know with certainly that God is about to do a miracle. We don't need to leave out the human elements of the story, nor do we need to exaggerate the God elements, because both aspects contain the prophetic word that every believer needs.

We must constantly be reminded of who we are in God and who God is in our lives, because that's what positions us to move with Him again today as He demonstrates His power in and through us. Our most profound distinction as the people of God is that He is present and active among us. He is our true inheritance and our exceedingly great reward.

Paul tells us that we see Him "in part" as we run the race of our lives on earth. But keeping the testimony trains us to look at life through the lenses of our history of God's supernatural invasions. Keeping the testimony keeps Him at the center of our lives.

CHAPTER 5

Memories
That Give Life

Jesus led His disciples into continuous experiences with the miraculous. Every occasion was designed to equip them for the next unexpected challenge they were to face and teach them the ways of His world, a world they couldn't see without help.

On one such occasion the twelve were in a life-threatening storm. The Gospel of Mark emphasizes that the storm was overwhelming to them only because their hearts were hard to the lessons from the previous miracle of the multiplication of the loaves and fishes (see Mark 6:52).

This is astonishing, because they were perfectly obedient in the previous situation. In fact, their obedience helped release the miracle, yet the hardness in their hearts prevented them from living from the testimony of their breakthrough into the challenge of a storm!

The implication of this is a bit sobering. We can obey, get the miracle, be thankful, give God all the glory, and yet be ill-equipped for the next challenge if the testimony does not become the lens through which we see reality. The disciples rejoiced in the outcome, but never learned from the process. The process was an integral part of the miracle.

When the disciples addressed the people's need for food, Jesus responded with this command: "You give them something to eat" (Mark 6:37). When they didn't know how, He never withdrew His command. He simply enabled them to do the impossible. Because they never realized that the food didn't multiply at Jesus' hands, but instead multiplied at theirs, they never learned the lesson that would give them courage in the storm.

Without this realization, they would never know that when Jesus commissioned them to go to the other side of the sea, it was the same as if He were in the boat with them. The commission enables us in the same way as His physical presence enables. A commission comes when we are in submission to His mission, resulting in the authority needed to carry out the mission.

And He left them, and getting into the boat again, departed to the other side. Now the disciples had forgotten to take bread, and they did not have more than one loaf with them in the boat. Then He charged them, saying, "Take heed, beware of the leaven of the Pharisees and the leaven of Herod."

And they reasoned among themselves, saying, "It is because we have no bread." But Jesus, being aware of it, said to them, "Why do you reason because you have no bread? Do you not yet perceive nor understand? Is your heart still hardened? Having eyes, do you not see? And having ears, do you not hear? And do you not remember? When I broke the five loaves for the five thousand, how many baskets full of fragments did you take up?" They said to Him, "Twelve."

"Also, when I broke the seven for the four thousand, how many large baskets full of fragments did you take up?" And they said, "Seven."

So He said to them, "How is it you do not understand?" (Mark 8:13-21).

MIRACLES CHANGE THE WAY WE "SEE"

The renewing of the mind allows the Spirit of God to shape our perception, and our minds become an instrument of righteousness.

Our history with God should shape our perception. In Mark 8:13-21, Jesus warned the disciples about the leaven of Herod and of the Pharisees. Leaven is the subtle influence on the mind to shape how we perceive reality. As they looked around the boat for food, Jesus asked them, "Why do you reason because you have no bread?" He was addressing their reasoning that was unaffected by their history with Him. Experiences with God are both wonderful and costly. He then took them back to two experiences He had with them in the multiplying of food and asked them if they remembered what happened when they fed the multitudes.

I return to this story on a regular basis to look at the questions Jesus asks because I must change, and I sense there are many answers for me in this event. The issues He dealt with are core issues in following Christ—especially for one who longs to release His miraculous power and glory into the world.

"Why do you reason because you have no bread?" It is as if Jesus asked His disciples, "Why does your reasoning start with what you don't have? Once I took you into the miracle of the multiplication of food, you lost the right to begin any pattern of thought with what you don't have."

Miracles erase options for the believer. This is what the renewed mind looks like. It no longer starts with lack. A miracle contains the spiritual nutrients that are to be released into our system to make us think like Christ. In this case they fortify us with grace to never start a train of thought with what we don't have. But as we see with the twelve, it is possible to be unaffected by the experience of a miracle.

I am very encouraged by a tremendous shift in perspective within the Church. But I am still convicted by this story in Mark. Too many times I am faced with a problem, and I think, "I don't have what it takes for that situation." Immediately I start looking at my resources as though I were the answer to my dilemma.

So Jesus took them through a series of questions. *"How is it that you don't perceive? Is your heart still hard?"* (paraphrase). When He takes us into the realm of miracles and we become exposed to the supernatural, it will alter the way we see reality—if our hearts are not hard. However, if our view of reality is not adjusted to accommodate ongoing miracles in our lives, then our heart is limiting the full effect of the nutrients being released in our system. Those nutrients are called "grace," which is divine enablement.

Jesus asked His disciples how many times they had to experience the miracle of supernatural provision in order to see from divine perspective. Jesus was talking about the perception of their legal access to a Kingdom that never ends and does not have limited resources. They were given a place of faith to see the limitless resource to draw from for any situation. Perhaps they knew the gift on them was for others, but they didn't see that it was also for them. Miracles are supposed to change our perspective on reality.

Jesus asked them, *"Having eyes, do you not see? And having ears, do you not hear? And do you not remember?"* This is where we can learn the most, and recover our losses, if we see the truth and truly repent. The clearest form of spiritual perception is *seeing,* the second is *hearing,* and the final one is *remembering.* Remembering is something that someone can learn to do through choice, and that in turn helps to develop spiritual sensitivities. It's as though we can choose to subject ourselves to the influence of the miraculous through biblical meditation and then brace ourselves for the supernatural result!

I am constantly looking around to see what God is doing. There are times that I can see it clearly, but there are times I am clueless. Once I was in Germany praying with leaders before a meeting and I had a snapshot picture come into my mind. It is the visual equivalent of the *still, small voice.* In the *snapshot* I saw someone to my right with arthritis in the spine. I said to her, "The Lord Jesus heals you." No one touched her—she was healed in the command.

So when the meeting began, I had the burning conviction to go after this. I started off by saying, "Someone here has arthritis in the spine." The person stood up and just as I saw in the prayer meeting, she was on my right. I declared over her, "The Lord Jesus heals you." She began to tremble as the fire of God's presence was on her, and I asked where her pain was and she replied, "It's impossible; it's impossible. It's gone; it's gone." She was healed right before our eyes. It happened because I could see. But more often than not, I don't see as clearly as this. If I can't see, I can usually still hear.

When I walked into a meeting in Dallas a few years ago, I heard the word "deafness" as I entered the sanctuary. Toward the end of that meeting I was reminded by the Spirit what I heard. Then an unusual anointing for healing came into the room, and 83 people were healed of some measure of deafness—from total deafness caused by a severed auditory nerve to various levels of deafness. I had never seen that many people healed of deafness in one meeting. And it all happened in about 15 minutes.

SEEING THROUGH OUR HISTORY

The encouraging thing is that if I can't see, and I can't hear, I can always remember. This is where "keeping the testimony" comes into play—I have to start thinking about what I have seen God do. His activities must become valuable enough to us that we store them in our thinking as we will probably have times where we need to *jump-start* our ability to hear and see. (My illustrations are unique because they have to do with leading public meetings, which not everyone has the responsibility to do, but the principles are transferable to every position in life.)

Often I'm in a situation where I need direction for a meeting, and I can't seem to see or hear. I automatically turn my attention to what I've seen Him do in the past. And almost always He duplicates the very miracles that come to my mind. Once I declare them, out of my history with God, they become present-tense realities affecting situations as the stories reveal the nature of God and His ways.

I search my heart and whatever comes to the surface first, whether it's deafness, broken bones, or injuries from accidents, I will have people stand. What am I doing? I am remembering and operating out of my history with God. It provides a new way of seeing my present situation. This has happened so many times that I now feel I have permission to call out certain conditions or diseases at any time and He will come and heal them. This flows from my history with God.

Every believer has experienced at least one miracle—your conversion. You've seen the transformation that took place in your life from the inside out. Begin to feed yourself on what God has done. It sets the framework within which to view coming problems. I frequently have people ask, "Have you ever seen anyone healed from __?" and they will name their condition. Why are they asking me? Because they know that if God did it once, He'll do it again. In so many words, they are asking to see if there is a testimony that has shaped my perspective on their problem.

I had a man come and ask me if I had ever seen a leg shrink. He had broken his leg 25 years earlier and when it healed it grew 1.5 inches past the other one. He had heard the stories of missing bone being replaced and legs growing out, but he was interested to know if we'd ever seen one shrink. (If I hadn't, there has to be a first time, so I would have gone after it anyway.)

However, after stopping to think, I recalled that I had seen it happen with a pastor who had been in a snowmobile accident. After he healed up he also had a leg that was too long. In an Italian restaurant in Sacramento, I asked the pastor to turn his chair sideways. I held his legs and commanded the long leg to shrink. It obeyed. When he returned to his physical therapist, the therapist told the pastor his legs were perfect.

Remembering that story enabled me to tell this man I had seen God do it. He was a contractor, and his long leg had been causing him back problems for many years. I asked him to sit down while I held his legs in my hands. Then I paused for a moment and a thought occurred to me, "Should I shrink the long leg or lengthen the shorter leg? Most people wouldn't mind being a little bit taller." I caught him (and myself) completely off guard when I said, "Right leg, grow in Jesus' name."

The right leg began to grow out slowly. Then all of a sudden it shot out past the other leg three or four inches and the guy screamed in pain! It was as though years of growing pains were hitting him all at once. On the outside I'm sure I looked very calm, but on the inside I was wondering, "What have I done! This guy thinks he hobbled in here...wait until he tries to walk out!"

I began to search my heart to figure how to pray when I remembered studying the word *shalom*. It means "peace." It has to be one of the most pregnant words in the Bible—filled with life and meaning. It means *soundness of mind, health, prosperity*—and most everything else we have ever prayed for is addressed by this word. I thought, "This situation has to be covered in that word." So I prayed, "And now Lord, just let the shalom of Heaven, your peace, rest upon this man." His right leg then shrank back to perfectly match the other one. He came to me the next day and said, "Bill, I've measured it every possible way, it's absolutely perfect." I celebrated with him.

Six months later I was in Rochester, Minnesota, where there was a girl who had had cancer in her leg. They had to remove a large piece of bone and replace it with a metal rod. They made it an inch and a half too long because she was only 15 years old and the doctors figured she would grow into that length. When I met her she was 27. And because she hadn't grown any more in those 12 years, she had problems with her back. She asked me to pray for her.

Because of my recent experience, for which God *covered me,* I took her leg and commanded the one with the metal rod to shrink. It yielded to the command. She came to me the next day and told me it was perfect. She then stated that she was glad I commanded the leg with the metal to shrink, because if the other grew in length the doctors would have told her, "See, we told you, you would grow into it."

When you listen to God, you look good even when you don't deserve it.

KEEPING A PERSONAL RECORD

Why do I share these stories? It is important that we remember our history with God. What is your history? Meditate on it. Record the miracles you see. Let that one discipline help you to develop the skills of hearing and seeing. Purposefully recording and rehearsing history is a step toward maturity in the gifts and the release of miracle power.

I just want to put this one tool in your hand. If you will use it, you will stay encouraged every day of your life, and you will have an important key for the renewing of your mind. The tool is the testimony. Let everything be tied to a reminder of God's supernatural interventions. Your *God history* needs to become a string of monuments that become reference points for the rest of your life. Had the disciples been sitting there meditating on the wonders of Jesus' ability to multiply food when He talked to them about the leaven of Herod and the Pharisees, they wouldn't have gone into fear mode about lunch.

CHAPTER 6

Courage to Leave
a Legacy

When God brought the children of Israel into the Promised Land, He gave them a very clear assignment—an assignment that prophetically illustrates the assignment we have as His children in the New Covenant.

The Israelites were to displace the pagan peoples living in their promised territory, spread their own tribes throughout it, and ultimately establish cities of refuge in each region.

Likewise, Christ commissioned us to go into our promised territory—all the world—and make disciples of the nations, displacing the influence of the kingdom of darkness and releasing the reality of the Kingdom of Heaven.

As it is for us, the Israelites' success in fulfilling each part of the assignment was entirely dependent on their ability to do that which God had been training them to do in the wilderness—to follow His manifest presence and do what He said, when He said to do it.

And upon what did their ability to follow His presence and obey His voice depend? God made the answer to this question clear to Joshua when He commissioned him to lead the Israelites in their assignment:

> *No man shall be able to stand before you all the days of your life; as I was with Moses, so I will be with you. I will not leave you nor forsake you. Be strong and of good courage, for to this people you shall divide as an inheritance the land which I swore to their fathers to give them. Only be strong and very courageous, that you may observe to do according to all the law which Moses My servant commanded you; do not turn from it to the right hand or to the left, that you may prosper wherever you go. This Book of the Law shall not depart from your mouth, but you shall meditate in it day and night, that you may observe to do according to all that is written in it. For then you will make your way prosperous, and then you will have good success. Have I not commanded you? Be strong and of good courage; do not be afraid, nor be dismayed, for the Lord your God is with you wherever you go (Joshua 1:5-9).*

THE MANDATE FOR COURAGE

We've already looked at what God meant when He told Joshua to meditate in the Book of the Law, but when we look at this injunction in context, we can see the greater significance of why keeping the testimony was the key to Israel's success in fulfilling their commission as a nation.

Interestingly, God set up Joshua's commission with the same promise He gave to Moses when Moses asked, "Who am I that I should go to Pharaoh, and that I should bring the children of Israel out of Egypt?" God simply answered, "I will certainly be with you" (Exod. 3:11-12).

Similarly, Jesus' final words in His Great Commission to us were, "I am with you always, even to the end of the age" (Matt. 28:20). The implication of this promise is twofold in that God's presence among us determines our identity and consequently, what we are able to accomplish.

But also we must develop a growing awareness of God's presence among us if we are to *draw* from that presence and walk out our God-given assignment. Our awareness of God is what determines how we respond to Him, how we perceive reality, and how we live. It is an extremely important element required for us to be successful in following and obeying God.

King David spoke of this provision when he said, "I have set the Lord always before me; because He is at my right hand I shall not be moved" (Ps. 16:8). The word *set* means to "place." We do play a role in making Him conspicuous. The revivalist Duncan Campbell described the element of overwhelming presence as the essence of the revival he experienced on the Hebrides Islands in the

1950s. He said that "an awareness of God"[1] filled the atmosphere in the region, creating an environment in which repentance, conversion, prayer, and worship naturally became the chief activities.

When we increase our awareness of God's presence, the commands that God gives us become more doable. "God with us" must become the platform for all of life. Joshua received a key principle of victory in the exhortation to "be strong and very courageous." This exhortation was obviously important, as God repeated it three times in the few sentences we read in Joshua 1:5-9. Great courage and strength would be needed "to do according to all the law which Moses...commanded" and not to "turn from it to the right hand or to the left" (Josh. 1:7).

But the final repetition is the most significant, because God makes a link between it and the promise. "Be strong and of good courage; do not be afraid, nor be dismayed, *for* the Lord your God is with you wherever you go" (Josh. 1:9). The truth He gave to Joshua and gives to us in this exhortation is simple but profound: *Our strength and courage to do what God has told us to do flow directly from our awareness that God is with us.*

An integral part of this way of life is the assignment to meditate on God's Word—the Law. In Joshua's case, the Book of the Law included Genesis, Exodus, Leviticus, Numbers, and Deuteronomy—the books of Moses. It included both the commands of the Lord and the whole history of His supernatural relationship with

Israel. In our case, we are to meditate in the record of God's commands and His miraculous interventions in human history, which includes the Scriptures primarily, along with the testimonies of the saints throughout history along with our own personal history with God.

In the immediate context of the command given to Joshua 1:5-9, God doesn't give Joshua a whole lot of explanation for how and why this meditation works. His point is that it does. He says *we* actually make our own way successful and prosperous by doing it. We've seen that the prophetic power of the testimony is one dimension of how it makes us prosper in our calling. However, from the larger context of Scripture I think we can also make a connection between the three elements we see in this passage, and that is that *our meditation on the testimonies of the Lord is the primary thing God has given us to sustain our awareness of His presence with us.* When we remember who He is and what He has done, the prophetic anointing on the testimony creates the awareness that He is with us now and is ready to do it again. That awareness is the source of our courage and strength.

The command to meditate on the testimonies of the Lord also clarifies how God defines our success in fulfilling our commission as His people. Our success is simply a matter of *radical obedience*. It's not about doing supernatural things; it's about doing what He's asked us to do. It's about our relational response to God.

Our connection with God is obviously the source of all blessing, prosperity, and goodness in our lives. We make our way prosperous through obedience because when we do what He asks us to do, we strengthen our connection with the source of life. The more completely our lives are in agreement with God, the more His nature and Kingdom manifest in us.

Radical obedience, because it's a matter of relationship, is always a heart issue. Thus keeping the testimony, the key to radical obedience, is designed first to do something in our hearts. Moses told the people, "Only *take heed to yourself, and diligently keep yourself*, lest you forget the things your eyes have seen, and *lest they depart from your heart* all the days of your life" (Deut. 4:9).

Later, Solomon said, "Keep your heart with all diligence, for out of it spring the issues of life" (Prov. 4:23). Whatever fills our hearts will fill our thinking and behavior. When we keep the testimony, we fill our hearts with *truth*—the truth of who God is, the truth of who we are, and the truth of where we've come from and where we're going in God. But it is *our* responsibility to fill our hearts with the truth, because if we don't, as we saw in the previous chapter, we allow our hearts to be filled with the lies of the enemy.

Throughout the Book of Deuteronomy, Moses emphasized to Israel that from God's perspective, the real threat to their success did not exist among the enemy tribes in the Promised Land or in any other external reality. The primary threat was the internal reality of their hearts. God said of them, "…It is a people who go astray in their hearts, and they do not know My ways" (Ps. 95:10). The words translated *go astray* in this verse means "to wander." Israel's wandering in the wilderness was really the outward manifestation of what was already in their hearts. In other words, our internal reality becomes our external reality. And as this verse explains, what was in their hearts was related to the fact that they did not know the *ways* of God.

Scripture points out that knowing God's ways is more than knowing God's *acts*. Psalm 103:7 says, "[The Lord] made known His ways to Moses, His acts unto the children of Israel." The revelation of God's ways is something that only comes to people who, like Moses, have a heart to know God, because only a heart like this is willing to pursue the God behind the acts.

We know that His acts reveal His ways. But in order to know His ways, we have to look at the acts of God like signs that point to something greater than themselves—the actual nature of God Himself. And unless we do, our ignorance of God's ways cannot help but leave us vulnerable to being led astray by our own hearts.

Meditating on the testimonies is all about following the signs to the One they point to. It is this responsibility, discipline, and passion to know God through the testimony that feeds and develops our awareness of His presence. It is an undeniable reality that He is a supernatural God who invades and overcomes impossibilities. Without the awareness of His presence with us, and without the understanding of His ways revealed in the testimony, we will not be able to consistently walk in radical obedience.

THE HIGH COST OF LOW COURAGE

The rest of Israel's history recorded in Scripture demonstrates this truth. The people of Israel did indeed break their covenant with God through disobedience. The following verses describe how this came to be:

So the people served the Lord all the days of Joshua, and all the days of the elders who outlived Joshua, who had seen all the great works of the Lord which He had done for Israel.... When all that generation had been gathered to their fathers, another generation arose after them who did not know the Lord, nor the work which He had done for Israel....and they forsook the Lord God of their fathers, who had brought them out of the land of Egypt; and they followed other gods from among the gods of the people who were all around them, and they bowed down to them; and they provoked the Lord to anger (Judges 2:7,10,12).

It is no mistake that the writer of Judges connects Israel's faithfulness to the Lord with remembering His *great works*. Asaph made the same correlation in Psalm 78:9-11:

The children of Ephraim, being armed and carrying bows,
Turned back in the day of battle.
They did not keep the covenant of God;
They refused to walk in His law,
And forgot His works
And His wonders that He had shown them.

What was it that the children of Ephraim lacked going into battle? The psalmist makes a point that they were outwardly prepared to face the enemy. What they lacked was something on the inside. I would propose that the psalmist orders his description in order to trace what they lacked back to its source. The source of the problem was that they forgot the works and wonders of God. They failed to keep the testimony. When they failed to keep the testimony, they forgot who they were, who God was, and what He required of them. They lacked awareness of His presence, and thus they lacked the understanding, strength, and courage to keep the covenant and walk in radical obedience.

When you walk in radical obedience, you have sustained confidence to face the difficulties of life. Radical obedience positions you for victory after victory because it preserves and expands your trust and intimacy with the God who makes you victorious. But when you're walking in disobedience, it's virtually impossible to muster the courage to face the battles around you.

The battles around us certainly look different from the battles Israel faced. Our enemy is a spiritual enemy, and our strategies and weapons are spiritual. But the nature of the battle is similar. Other people were living in the land that God had promised to His people. The circumstances directly contradicted the word God had spoken.

On a daily basis, every one of us likewise is faced with circumstances in our world that contradict what God has said about who we are and what we can and must do as co-laborers in bringing Heaven to earth. But the greater reality for us, as it was for Israel, is that God has equipped and positioned us for victory in these contradictions.

Because of this, God actually leads us into these circumstances! We are not playing defense in life; we are playing offense. In other words, we are not merely protecting what God has given us; we are seeking to advance in every area. We have superior power, superior strategies, and superior weapons. But while God positions and equips us, He will not force us to advance against the enemy, because only when we are co-laborers can we have co-ownership of the victory and the spoils. It is our privilege and responsibility to use what God has given us to take possession of what He has promised to us.

However, our success in the battle is determined by what we do before the battle begins. To put it another way, our success in the battles around us is determined by our success in the battles we all face in bringing our lives into submission to God. The word *radical* means "going to the root or origin." Radical obedience to God means refusing to compromise or redefine what He originally told us to do in order to fit within the paradigm of human possibility.

For example, it's common for believers to read Jesus' command to preach the Gospel of the Kingdom, heal the sick, raise the dead, cleanse the lepers, and cast out demons and think, "Well, I might be able to preach the Gospel. But God is the only one who does all those other things. I'll pray for the sick, but I can't heal them."

But Jesus didn't say to pray for the sick. He said to heal them. Radical obedience refuses to change what God says and instead addresses the areas in which our lives do not yet express God's standard by contending through prayer and stepping out in faith to do what God said.

Radical obedience is what brings victory inside of us, because it replaces un-renewed patterns of thinking and behavior with those of the Kingdom. It establishes our perspective and lifestyle on the premise that everything in the Christian life is actually impossible for those who have not been resurrected by the Spirit of God but is supernaturally possible for those who have. It trains us to see and believe that nothing is impossible.

It is this perspective that enables us to hold nothing back from God, to live passionately and sacrificially in our daily lives. And unless we have already embraced this sacrificial lifestyle before God, we will not have the ability to endure and overcome the contradictions into which He leads us. Unless we are walking in radical obedience, we will not make radical efforts in battle. We will back out of them.

One night a teenager was brought into one of our church meetings with a serious bone fracture. I was called over to pray, and when I saw how bad it was, I made a choice. I told them to go to the emergency room. Now, if I had never seen a broken bone healed in my life, this response would have been reasonable. But I had seen many bones instantly healed.

My response to this situation was illegal because of what I knew. I forgot what I had seen, so I lost sight of the presence of God and lacked the courage to face this impossibility. As this situation demonstrates, forgetting what God has done costs not only us but also those around us. The victories that God wants us to achieve are not just for our benefit. If we withdraw from the battle, we are actually costing people the blessings God wants to give them.

The weight of this responsibility should impress us with the importance of keeping the testimony as a lifestyle. Unless we are consistent to keep what God has done in our memories and conversations, a downward spiral begins to happen in our lives. The less we talk about the miraculous interventions of God, the lower our expectation to see them break out around us goes. The lower our expectation, the less we step into opportunities to minister to people. The less we minister to people, the less frequently we are exposed to the miracles of God around us. The less we're exposed to the miraculous, the less we talk about the miraculous…and the spiral can continue until eventually we lack any faith to see breakthrough in our circumstances, even when we've seen the very same impossibilities overcome by the power of God. We end up like the children of Ephraim, being fully armed but retreating from the battle. And the people who God desired to benefit from our breakthrough, the people to whom we owe an authentic re-presentation of Jesus, are robbed of their encounters.

LIVING UN-OFFENDED

As we saw in the previous chapter, keeping the testimony as a lifestyle comes down to the issue of remembering, particularly, remembering the right things. Our memories will make us cowardly or courageous. I've found that our memories either center on what God has done and is doing, or they center on what He hasn't done.

Time and time again I encounter Christians who are carrying around the memories of what God hasn't done. Many of them have been dealing with long-term illnesses. When they come to me for prayer they'll say, "I've been prayed for a thousand times. I've had so-and-so lay hands on me and prophesy my healing. I'm still not healed."

The first thing I'll address is the fact that, by keeping a record of what God hasn't done for them, they have actually built a case against God. This works to justify their own unbelief and positions them to be filled with offense over another unanswered prayer.

Unbelief and offense are two of the biggest hindrances to the miraculous. So I'll say to them, "I'll only pray for you if you agree to think of this as the very first time you've received prayer for this illness." The Bible says "now is the day of salvation" (2 Cor. 6:2). If I can get them to forget what God hasn't done and remind them of who He is, it can create an opening for them to receive what God wants to do for them.

Other Christians are holding God on trial, not for their own healing or breakthrough, but for a miracle in someone else's life. They're hanging their faith on a single event rather than on the God who has already purchased every miracle that everyone on the planet needs. Doing this not only perverts and weakens their faith; it, once again, effectively robs the other people around them from a true representation of God.

With these folks, I simply encourage them to stop praying only for one miracle and start stepping out to see what God wants to do all around them. I tell them to start collecting testimonies of other breakthroughs. What happens is that by putting their trust in the Lord and stepping out in radical obedience in other areas, these believers receive a greater anointing that will ultimately benefit the situation they were originally fixated upon.

Once again, the anointing that flows through our lives is always determined by our hearts. We will broker the world that our hearts are anchored to. If our hearts are anchored to the issue of what He hasn't done, if that is what we feed on, then we will broker that world, regardless of how religious we try to be in public. We will impart the grace of offense to people around us.

But if we are devoted to feeding our hearts on what God has done, the gratitude in our hearts will give us grace to endure the things we have no answers for. When people ask us why such and such hasn't happened, the grace that comes from celebrating God will enable us to respond, "I don't know. All I know is that as long as I feed myself on what He has done, I do just great."

We don't allow ourselves to stumble over a question that God isn't answering at the moment. Disappointment with God is a trap that will effectively suck the strength and courage from us and invite destruction into our lives. And disappointment almost always gets in when we allow what *isn't* happening to arrest our focus.

For this reason, if I'm praying for someone with an injured joint, for example, and that person still has pain when she moves it, I don't allow myself to focus on that. I work to position myself to find out what God is doing in the situation. I work to remember the testimony, because it helps me to build a case for healing, rather than building a case against it.

I realize that it can be hard for people to work on building a case for healing before they've experienced their own breakthrough. But the truth is that our greatest victories in God are usually built on the rubble of our greatest failures and disappointments. At Bethel we've now collected several testimonies of babies who were resurrected and safely delivered after having been confirmed dead in the womb by doctors. The story we don't often tell is that, some years ago, the wife of one of our elders had a baby who died in the womb. We prayed and felt we had a word from the Lord that it would live. We prophesied life over the baby. But the baby was born dead, and there was no resurrection. It rocked the whole church.

We also see cancer healed all the time in Redding and have a promise from God that we're passionately pursuing to create a cancer-free zone. But over the years, some of our dearest friends and family, including my own father, have died from cancer. In these situations, we did everything we knew to do. We prayed, fasted, prophesied, and declared the word of the Lord.

In the end, we had to make a choice regarding what we were going to believe about God in the face of this contradiction. We had to come back to the truth that the problem was still on our end. The problem is never on God's end. He is good, and He hasn't changed. And then, we had to make a choice about how we were going to respond to this truth. The enemy would try to use this truth to convince us to quit. But we took our pain, our frustration with our own lack, and our conviction that God still had more for us and allowed them to drive us to God with a desperate cry for breakthrough. We got back up on the horse and in the face of defeat, continued to step out and pray for people who needed those same breakthroughs. If we hadn't resolved to move forward with radical obedience to the will of God revealed in the testimony, I know that we would never have gained the great victories that eventually came to us.

For clarification, when I say that the problem is on our end, it doesn't imply that God was disappointed with us or somehow at odds with us. It doesn't imply that we had misheard what God had said, were being disobedient, or that what we did was entirely ineffective. It just means that the problem is part of the reality of living in a world that still does not express the will of God on earth as it is in Heaven.

Ultimately, we don't understand all the reasons that things turned out the way they did. Correctly responding to that kind of mystery is one of the most difficult challenges in the Christian life. It's in that place that the accuser of the brethren often finds an open door to try to convince us that what God has said about who we are and what we are called to accomplish is untrue and impossible. In these situations, we must remember the statement of Revelation 12:10-11:

Then I heard a loud voice saying in heaven, "Now salvation, and strength, and the kingdom of our God, and the power of His Christ have come, for the accuser of our brethren, who accused them before our God day and night, has been cast down. And they overcame him by the blood of the Lamb and by the word of their testimony, and they did not love their lives to the death."

We overcome the accuser by the word of our testimony. In other words, we don't overcome the accuser by focusing on what we don't know. We overcome him by standing on what we do know. The blind man in John chapter 9 demonstrates this wonderfully:

So they again called the man who was blind, and said to him, "Give God the glory! We know that this Man is a sinner." He answered and said, "Whether He is a sinner or not I do not know. One thing I know: that though I was blind, now I see." Then they said to him again, "What did He do to you? How did He open your eyes?" He answered them, "I told you already, and you did not listen. Why do you want to hear it again? Do you also want to become His disciples?" Then they reviled him and said, "You are His disciple, but we are Moses' disciples. We know that God spoke to Moses; as for this fellow, we do not know where He is from." The man answered and said to them, "Why, this is a marvelous thing, that you do not know where He is from; yet He has opened my eyes! Now we

know that God does not hear sinners; but if anyone is
a worshiper of God and does His will, He hears him.
Since the world began it has been unheard of that
anyone opened the eyes of one who was born blind. If
this Man were not from God, He could do nothing."
They answered and said to him, "You were completely
born in sins, and are you teaching us?" And they cast
him out (John 9:24-34).

It is clear from this passage that this formerly blind man was a keeper of the testimony. His knowledge of history had given him such a revelation of the ways of God that he immediately saw what the sign of his own miracle pointed to—the identity of Jesus Christ. He was also able to ignore the religious leaders' accusations simply because they went beyond the boundaries of what he knew. The reality of what he did know—that he was once blind, and now could see—was undeniable and eclipsed everything else in importance. By sticking to what he did know, his testimony, he effectively resisted the accusers and, as the rest of the story tells us, ended up in another face-to-face encounter with Christ that brought him even more fully into what God had for him.

"GOD WITH US"

By filling us with strength and courage, sustaining and increasing our awareness of God, and continually leading us into further encounters with God, keeping the testimony sets us on an upward spiral in God, just as surely as failing to keep it sets us on the downward spiral.

The truth is that we are heading in one or the other of these directions on a daily basis. It can take only a few moments for bad news or a contradiction of some kind to arrest our focus and diminish our strength. In the same way, we can be filled with courage and strength by taking a few moments to remember a testimony.

Keeping the testimony is at the heart of our spiritual health. In the same way that we feed, clothe, and exercise our bodies, keeping the testimony is something we must do as a lifestyle to keep us in a constant state of readiness—readiness to step into the next part of the lifelong assignment that God has given us. Our readiness, as we've seen, is determined by our awareness of the presence of God with us. When we keep the testimony, our sustained awareness of His presence enables us to respond to our circumstances from a renewed perspective.

Some time ago I was ministering in a church of about 250 people. Around 40 people were healed during the meeting, so I had them come up to give the testimonies of their healings. I went down the line and interviewed them, and at the end of the line was a gentleman who pointed to his nose and started to explain that the polyps that had been there were now gone. As soon as he pointed to his nose, the phrase "deviated septum" flashed through my mind, along with several testimonies of this condition being healed that I had personally witnessed.

Because I recognized the present anointing on that testimony, I immediately responded by interrupting the gentleman and telling everyone with a deviated septum to stand up, put their fingers on their noses, and receive healing. As soon as I did so, about six or eight people were instantly healed. One woman was weeping profoundly because she had been scheduled for surgery the next week to fix the problem.

A week later I was in another meeting sharing this testimony and there happened to be a woman sitting on the front row whose daughter had problems with a deviated septum and her sinuses. She started praying for her daughter as I was talking. She didn't know that as soon as I had said the phrase "deviated septum," her daughter had walked into the meeting. The daughter hadn't heard any of my teaching on the prophetic power of the testimony, but when she heard the phrase, her condition was instantly healed.

I love these stories and am awed by them because it is so obvious that God deserves all the credit for performing these miracles. But on the other hand, if I hadn't leaned into what had flashed across my spirit and declared a simple phrase, I believe that the anointing on that testimony for that particular condition would not have been released in the way it was. It happened so fast that I easily could have missed the moment.

It is for moments such as these that God desires us to learn to steward our inheritance of the testimony. He has given us this vast resource so that we can live every day encouraged, and so that we respond to every situation in our lives with a strong awareness of the One who is with us, the One who invades the impossible. And when we as a people begin to live from the conviction that nothing is impossible, I know we will begin to see the fruit of victory in our internal and external battles.

The true fruit of victory is transformation, the reality of Heaven coming to earth. In the next chapter we will see that the testimony is not only the key to victory, but to occupying the territory God has promised to us and bringing the transformational reality of the Kingdom of God into every segment of our cities and nations.

ENDNOTE

1. Sermon titled, "When the Heavens Flowed Down" http://www.openheaven.com/library/history/lewis.html.

CHAPTER 7

Living Under
the Influence

The purpose of God's wondrous stories is to draw us into the passionate pursuit of more of His presence. His intention is to draw us to live under the influence of His presence rather than simply obeying His principles. He has called us to Himself through His kindness, as it's the kindness of God that leads us to repentance. Experiencing complete forgiveness and having our minds renewed results in deep affection and intimacy. This is the bedrock for ongoing Kingdom experiences.

The Kingdom of God and the presence of God are inseparable. He works to anchor our affection for Him in the reality of His rule. This is His idea of true maturity, and we must pursue it. He has made it possible through great teaching, impartation prayer, and challenging opportunities to see the great impact of the Gospel of the Kingdom on our world.

We have many spiritual gifts, but for the most part they remain embryonic in form. It's not that they have no present purpose or effect. They do. A person is as likely to see cancer healed in his or her first miracle as a headache. Undeveloped things in the Kingdom still have the life of the King in them. Remember, the crumbs from the table that the Syrophoenican woman spoke of are powerful enough to bring healing and deliverance (see Matt. 7:28). The smallest measure of faith can move a mountain. By *embryonic,* I simply mean that these gifts are alive, but they're small and not fully formed. The Lord desires us to fan them into flame and become mature.

Gifts are free, but maturity is expensive. There are moments when the gifts of God explode and come into great fruition through one simple act of courage and boldness. In other words, what we thought would take years to grow sometimes grows in an instant. But the climate must be right—the climate of great faith, courage, and boldness. This is what happened to the apostle Paul.

Before God changed Paul's name, he was called Saul. In writing the Book of Acts, Luke always listed him second to Barnabas, saying "Barnabas and Saul." But the day came when extraordinary courage would be needed. An occultist named Elymas rose up against the pair to undermine the work of the Gospel and deceive potential converts. Boldness from the Holy Spirit came upon Paul to confront this devil.

But Elymas the magician (for thus his name is translated) was opposing them, seeking to turn the proconsul away from the faith. But Saul, who was also known as Paul, filled with the Holy Spirit, fixed his gaze on him, and said, "You who are full of all deceit and fraud, you son of the devil, you enemy of all righteousness, will you not cease to make crooked the straight ways of the Lord? And now, behold, the hand of the Lord is upon you, and you will be blind and not see the sun for a time." And immediately a mist and a darkness fell upon him, and he went about seeking those who would lead him by the hand (Acts 13:8-11 NASB).

Through one act of boldness Saul helped create the atmosphere where increase was released over his life. Soon afterward he received a name change to *Paul*, as well as a promotion. From that point on Luke mentions this apostolic duo as Paul and Barnabas.

Courage in the moment was all that was needed to unleash the potential that was lying dormant in Paul. Boldness became the catalytic ingredient that released the immediate promotion. Isn't it amazing that Paul drew from his own testimony for this manifestation of the Kingdom? He himself had received a rebuke from Jesus that resulted in short-term blindness. He'd seen that miracle and knew that God would do it again.

Many of us have waited for years for certain gifts to manifest, when the gift itself is waiting for the atmospheric shift to take place in the heart of the believer. This happens when the internal world of our spirit rises to meet the challenge of the external world. Paul's act of boldness was such a moment that brought about the necessary change. Bold faith can do the same for us.

EVERYONE IS A LEADER

The role of every believer is one of leadership. Not every person has a position with a title, but all lead. In fact, the day is coming when the nations of the world will stream to the people of God to hear what God is saying (see Mic. 4:2 and Isa. 2:2,3).

Jesus taught us that it is natural for all believers to know His voice, so it is equally natural to be able to tell others what He is saying. The author of Hebrews sought to affirm the leadership assignment for all Christians in saying, "By this time they ought to be teachers" (Heb. 5:12). The Holy Spirit has been given to every believer, making it possible for every believer to have a significant role in bringing transformation to individuals, cities, and nations.

There will always be generals in the army. But a private in the New Testament army has access to more than the generals of the Old Testament army did. Jesus made the point by saying that the "least in the Kingdom of heaven is greater than [John]" (Matt. 11:11).

The least person in the *Holy Spirit-filled life* has access to more in God than the greatest of all the Old Testament prophets. That is why each believer must think of him or herself as one who has influence as a leader. Doing so shifts our priorities and changes how we learn, what we think we need to learn, and how we process the challenges before us.

OUR RESPONSIBILITY

It is interesting to note that the greatest responsibility for us as leaders has nothing to do with leading. It has to do with following. I am designed to live under the influence of the King and His Kingdom, and I must make sure the right things impact me so that my impact on the world around me is what God intended. In doing so I must ensure that it is the works of the Lord that impact me most, for history testifies that the ongoing effect is an increased supernatural invasion of the Kingdom of God.

> *So the people served the Lord all the days of Joshua, and all the days of the elders who outlived Joshua, who had seen all the great works of the Lord which He had done for Israel. ...When all that generation had been gathered to their fathers, another generation arose after them who did not know the Lord, nor the work which He had done for Israel....and they forsook the Lord God of their fathers, who had brought them out of the land of Egypt; and they followed other gods from among the gods of the people who were all around them, and they bowed down to them;*

and they provoked the Lord to anger (Judges 2:7,10,12).

This is so simple and yet deeply profound: whenever Israel had leaders who had been exposed to the works of God, the nation had a heart to know and follow God. The same principle is repeated in Joshua 24:31 that we might never forget it!

There is a pronounced influence upon those who have witnessed the supernatural—that which they cannot control, explain, or understand. The result is wonderful; it draws them to the One who does wonders. There is another implication from this verse, equally profound: when their leaders either did not remain conscious of the supernatural interventions of God or worse yet, had never seen them, the people they served did not follow God. The results of both are devastating.

It is unlikely that the generation of leaders that came after the Joshua/elder group had a calculated plan to lead Israel away from God. Coldness of heart and rebellion don't usually come suddenly. But the absence of miracles seldom produces a life of radical obedience to God.

Furthermore, consider this: nearly every great leader of the Bible experienced the miraculous and/or supernatural—yet many Christians try to live without them. Exposure to the supernatural works of God changes the capacity of leaders to lead, thereby changing the bent of the people of God to pursue Him.

Such exposure is the equivalent of a spiritual change of DNA. Something is altered in that person that enables him or her to lead in such a way that the people of God inherit a heart for God through that leader's influence. True apostolic leadership always empowers rather than controls, and empowering a passion for God is one of the most necessary, yet often least cultivated skills, a spiritual leader possesses.

In the absence of miracles, something else happened in the Old Testament that is beyond coldness of heart. They went past that. Judges 2:12 says they "forsook" God. This implies that there was a deliberate turning from the God of Israel.

Leaders create atmosphere, either good or bad. True spiritual leaders are those who carry their own Heaven-centered *spiritual weather system* that permeates their realm of influence and authority. When leaders live under the atmosphere of Heaven, their exposure to miracles (which is Heaven's atmosphere on earth) changes their capacity to bring the people of God into their supernatural potential.

ALL ORDER EXISTS TO PROMOTE LIFE

I believe the model for biblical government is found in the family. When the fathers and mothers have a tendency toward a form of religion without power, their descendants seldom have the motivation to pay the price necessary to carry on their family's legacy of righteousness.

But when the model of purpose, passion, *and* power form the nature of that home or church, the next generation is more likely to rise in the midst of the darkness of world circumstances with a torch declaring the purposes of God on the earth. Mothers and fathers, both natural and spiritual, must arise with purpose, passion, and courage that they might partner in the wonder of His supernatural activities on the earth.

The fault for Israel's lack of the supernatural manifestations lies not only with the generation who were unexposed to miracles. It actually rests squarely on the shoulders of the parents who had seen the miracles for themselves but didn't pay the price necessary for them to continue.

Joshua received a supernatural lifestyle from Moses as an inheritance. An inheritance is something we get for free that someone else paid a price for. But if we don't pay a price to increase what we got for free, there'll be nothing to leave to the next generation.

It is ironic that the Joshua generation had enough influence to perpetuate righteousness without the ongoing experience of miracles. But the generations could not sustain righteousness without stepping into the realm of power that the testimony was calling them into. This reveals responsibility to do more than memorize stories for stories' sake. They must launch us into greater personal encounters with the God of wonders until those wonders happen around us. The testimony is to make us hungry for more, giving us the license to pursue super-natural breakthroughs.

A life without power has results that are disastrous. In the absence of the supernatural invasions of God there arose a generation that had no compass. Their wandering and eventual rebellion exploded in the absence of exposure to the God of wonders. It is required of each of us to live in such a way that God has to show up to sustain us. Reducing Christianity to what is humanly possible is responsible for the cold-hearted condition of many generations throughout history. Moral teaching, while absolutely necessary, seldom lights a fire in the hearts of a generation that was born to "take a bullet" for an eternal purpose. People by nature thrive on cause and purpose. The Church was never meant to be known for its disciplines. We are to be known for our passions. We must burn with renewed passion for Him and Him alone!

CONTINUALLY EXPOSED TO MIRACLES

The responsibility of every leader in the Church is to become exposed, and *remain* exposed, to the miracles of God and the God of miracles. Sincerity and genuine concern for the people of God are important but cannot take the place of such exposure.

The transformation that takes place in and through the church because of the increase of supernatural activities does not happen just because spiritual leaders are reading some of the excellent books on Christian leadership. What is needed cannot be found through reading alone. It must come through exposure to the miracle realm. Nor will such a change happen by merely refining our leadership priorities to help bring out the best in others. Nothing can replace the transformation made possible through exposure to the glory of God through miracles. We owe it to those around us to do whatever is necessary to be impacted over and over again through God's miraculous activities on the earth. The rewards are priceless. The cost for this neglect is eternal.

In years past many of my friends have traveled to Africa and Latin America on a regular basis for ministry just to stay exposed to the God who still does wonders. (That miracles have been easier and more common in those cultures is no secret.) They refused to live under the smallness of the North American religious culture that worked to create an image of God that could be controlled and reduced to words. Such a mind-set whittles Him down to our size; the near absence of miracles has been the result.

Thankfully that is changing. We now see extraordinary miracles in North America more frequently. I'd like to suggest that at least part of the reason for this was the continued effort by a great number of leaders who did whatever was necessary to stay exposed to, and impacted by, the God of wonders. The increasing passion in the Church for the "more" of the Gospel of the Kingdom is the result.

As I have worked to declare the testimonies of God's supernatural interventions, miracles have followed. And I have watched as great numbers of believers who had given little thought to a life of miracles have done *an about-face*. They have become infected with a passion for more of God when they never even appeared to be likely candidates for this lifestyle. After being exposed to the God who only does wondrous things, they tell me that they now know why they are alive. That's a pretty strong statement from one who only moments earlier had no passion whatsoever.

Exposure is the key. When people who are truly born again become exposed to a genuine work of the Spirit of God, they suddenly rise to a purpose and call they never thought possible. This is the normal Christian life. And leaders who become exposed, expose. And so the nature of church life is changed.

What's even more thrilling is that unbelievers also find their call and purpose in meeting the God of wonders. Some of our people overheard a conversation at a table next to them in a local restaurant. The woman at the table had cancer and had come to Redding to be healed. They offered to pray for her at her table. When they did, a demon manifested, creating quite a scene. They handled this situation quite discreetly, working to protect the dignity of the woman whom Jesus was setting free.

Yet people noticed, as it was in the middle of the restaurant. The manager saw that one of his waitresses was explaining to others what was happening. He then asked her if she attended Bethel Church where the people who prayed came from. When she said yes, he began to confess his sins to her. The power and compassion being evidenced in his restaurant drew a line in the sand that forced him to make a decision. He was exposed to power, and his heart was revealed.

If I am not filled with wonder, am I really positioned to say He is wonderful? If I am not filled with power, am I really positioned to say He is powerful? Where I have set the eyes of my heart will determine the reality that I release around me.

Heaven is filled with perfect trust in God, and this earth is filled with mistrust. We will always reflect the nature of the world we are most aware of.

Signs that make us wonder help to bring about a change in the heart and disposition of the Church. Exposure to the God of miracles is not the only thing necessary for bringing about reformation. But neither is it optional. This is what makes developing a culture that feeds on the testimony so powerful, and so necessary.

CHAPTER 8

The Power of Transformation

I truly believe that the sustained outpouring of the miraculous in which we have been privileged to participate is directly connected to the value we place on the testimony. It helps us to keep an awareness of God's supernatural interventions, which in turn affects our conversations. Israel's success was connected to what they thought about and what they talked about (see Josh. 1:8). We naturally reproduce whatever we dwell on.

We have established a practice of beginning every one of our weekly staff meetings and monthly board meetings with a time of recounting the testimonies of what God has done in the preceding days. At least half of our meeting time is devoted to sharing stories of the miraculous, which usually amounts to one to two hours of just testimonies. These stories include miracles of healing, deliverances, conversions, encounters, and even how God is working in our children and restoring families and marriages. I even hired someone to record the testimonies to help us place the proper value on His supernatural interventions among man. We consider this just as much our "business" as everything else we are responsible for.

Testimonies keep us encouraged and aware. It is simply impossible to sit through an hour and a half of hearing how Heaven has been invading earth all over our city and the world and go away discouraged. When we share these stories, we are releasing the anointing of the spirit of prophecy over one another, saying, "This is our God. This is what He's like. This is what He's doing, and this is what He's going to do." It gives us grace to face whatever impossibilities we are currently facing.

Sadly, it is possible to lose a sense of awe and gratitude for the miraculous. It is almost hard to imagine, but Israel grumbled frequently to God in the wilderness in spite of the fact that every day for 40 years they experienced divine health, manna on the ground, and shoes that didn't wear out—plus the visible sign of God's presence among them with the cloud and pillar of fire.

We are in danger of this same complacency when we don't cultivate a heart of thankfulness and expectation. If we are unimpressed with miracles, it is a warning sign that we are allowing bitterness, unbelief, or the hardening of our hearts toward God. Or we have simply stopped being thankful for what God is doing and allowed ourselves to set our hearts on what He isn't doing.

Another common mistake is to become more wrapped up with the signs than with the One the signs are pointing to. When this happens, we start to evaluate miracles according to human criteria where we categorize them according to difficulty, forgetting that in ourselves we have no more power to heal a headache than to heal leukemia.

With such affinity for entertainment value tied directly to the seriousness of a disease, it takes more and more difficult situations to make us thankful and rejoicing. In this case AIDS or cancer miracles bring a shout of praise, but the pinched nerve in the back being healed is treated as mundane, bringing little response.

Our joy should not depend on the size of the problem but on the actual invasion of Heaven. I've seen thousands of miracles in my life, and some of them have been more dramatic than others. But the truth is I am responsible to celebrate the goodness of God in all of them.

As long as we steward our hearts before the Lord and allow His works to point us to Him, we will find that His works cannot fail to inspire awe, thanks, and celebration. And when I can be trusted to steward my heart in the seemingly simple things, I become qualified for the more critical.

Keeping the testimony in our conversation also fills our hearts and minds with the revelation of God, creating a heightened awareness of His presence and His ways. This revelation trains our minds and hearts to perceive our circumstances from Heaven's perspective.

When I focus my attention on what God has done and is doing, I remain or become thankful. That one attitude of the heart changes my impact on the world around me, perhaps more than any other. It is that one characteristic that enables me to live aware of God.

Without a sustained awareness of the God who invades the impossible, I will reduce ministry to what I can accomplish with my ministry gifts. These gifts are like sails on a boat—without the wind, they're useless. We all need the wind of God to breathe on what we are gifted to do so that those gifts become eternally effective. If we fail to regularly *remember* who God is, what He has done, and what He is going to do, we *will* make decisions on the basis of what we can accomplish without Him, which restricts us to a life of the "possible." This leads to discouragement, small vision, mediocrity, burnout, and all the other problems that plague Christian leaders who lose touch with what God is doing.

THE GOLDEN AGE

This approach to creating a Kingdom culture is not new. We are taking our cue from two of the most successful leaders of history, David and Solomon.

In my opinion there has been only one time in the entire history of Israel when a godly leader was succeeded by another godly leader (albeit one who, partly because of a lack of ongoing exposure to supernatural power, later made disastrous choices) who built on his father's legacy and brought the nation into such a level of blessing and peace that it inspired awe and honor from the leaders of neighboring nations.

What did these men possess that enabled them to lead Israel into their Golden Age? Solomon's account in Proverbs reveals one of his father's passions—something he groomed his son from childhood to seek more than anything else: wisdom. But where did David's passion for wisdom come from? How did he discover this key to successful leadership? Consider his following statements:

> *The testimony of the Lord is sure, making wise the simple* (Psalm 19:7).

Wisdom was David's portion from the testimony. Another Psalmist added to this insight with the following statement on the influence of the testimony.

> *Your testimonies also are my delight and my counselors* (Psalm 119:24).

> *I have more understanding than all my teachers, for your testimonies are my meditation* (Psalm 119:99).

TESTIMONIES COUNSEL THE HEART

David's passion for the testimony of God positioned him for access to stunning encounters and revelation. His wisdom to rule came from the same source. David took counsel in the testimonies of the Lord and discovered that they gave him access to deeper wisdom and understanding than the "seasoned" counselors around him.

In the same way, testimonies are to give counsel to us. Every day there are situations that arise requiring us to make decisions. As believers, our focus and desire are to be directed toward doing what God is doing in these situations. Testimonies help us make these decisions by revealing God's previous supernatural interventions. And because the testimony by its nature is something that God is ready to "do again," we can make our decision based on His intention to repeat the miracle. We have seen Him heal cancer many times. Those testimonies counsel us to command the cancer in front of us to leave and for the body to be healed.

Testimonies also counsel us by revealing the nature of God and the principles of how He moves. They anchor core truths in our thinking so that we can see impossible situations from Heaven's perspective with conviction.

Our resolve to grow in the knowledge of Him and His ways is the key to wisdom. Real wisdom is not something you can get apart from relationship with God. Hebrew wisdom was not theoretical in nature: rather, it was the ability to make godly choices. The wise man wants to live to please God. Solomon stated: "The Lord gives wisdom" (Prov. 2:6). It is possible to honor certain Kingdom principles and experience in measure the results God promised, but without discovering God's wisdom contained in relationship, no one can experience life as God *intended*.

"The Lord by wisdom founded the earth; by understanding He established the heavens" (Prov. 3:19). The realm of God's wisdom contains the blueprint and design for every aspect of creation, what life on earth *ought to be*. We can't separate the wisdom of God from God Himself; His wisdom is the expression of His character, nature, will, and desires.

Solomon discovered the nature of wisdom and likened Him to a person. He wrote about this Person who speaks several times throughout the Book of Proverbs. Hear what Wisdom has to say in chapter 8:

> *The Lord possessed me at the beginning of His way,*
> *Before His works of old. I have been established from*
> *everlasting,*
> *From the beginning, before there was ever an earth....*
> *When He marked out the foundations of the earth,*
> *Then I was beside Him as a master craftsman;*
> *And I was daily His delight,*
> *Rejoicing always before Him,*
> *Rejoicing in His inhabited world,*
> *And my delight was with the sons of men* (Proverbs 8:22-23; 29-31).

Here we see the multiple dimensions of God's personality interacting with each other and through their intimacy and delight in one another, creating the entire universe. We see that the person of Wisdom, as identified in First Corinthians 1:30, created us and our world. He was driven by the expression of joy.

We came from joy, and we were made for joy. Any plan for life that does not involve our being perpetually joyful is in contradiction to God's design for us. In the last four phrases of this passage is a parallelism that compares God's relationship to Wisdom and our relationship to Wisdom. The same two words are used to describe both relationships—"delight" and "rejoicing." God has designed us for the same kind of relationship that He has with Wisdom—a relationship of mutual joy and delight, and therefore a relationship of co-creating.

CREATING

The Golden Age of David and Solomon foreshadows our role of co-creating with God. Solomon brought into fruition and demonstration much of what his father had taught him. He did so by nothing other than the wisdom that he had been taught to seek from the Lord.

Solomon declared, "Through wisdom a house is built, and by understanding it is established" (Prov. 24:3). In light of Proverbs 8, we might rephrase this to say that it is through co-creating with the Spirit of Wisdom that a house is established. That Hebrew word translated *house* can refer to a family, a home, a temple, a city, or even a nation.

Solomon, the one who wrote of and experienced a relationship of delight and co-creating with Wisdom, is best known for the houses he built and established—the Lord's house, the king's house (both home and family), and the house of Israel.

Divine wisdom is not distinguished by the stoic, dry, conservative traits that many associate with it. In Proverbs 8, divine wisdom has celebration and rejoicing at its core, is inherently expressive, happy, and above all, creative. In verse 12, Wisdom declares, "I wisdom dwell with prudence, and find out knowledge of witty inventions" (Prov. 8:12 KJV).

Religious solutions to the world's problems are usually anything but creative. They generally stifle all expression of creativity and joy, but the expressions of divine wisdom that we are called to demonstrate are creative and life-giving in nature. They are not focused on controlling the world but on freeing it from bondage so that it can experience the blessing and prosperity of Heaven.

Under Solomon's rule, Israel was not known for the great military they had, or for the sophistication of their penal or welfare systems. Nor were they known merely by what they lacked—the lack of enemies or the lack of disease—but for the presence of peace and abundance among them. The solutions that divine wisdom brings do not simply get rid of problems, but also establish excellence, blessing, and increase in places where it didn't exist.

It isn't simply the greatness and splendor of the temple and royal palace but the prosperity and godliness that pervaded the entire society under Solomon's leadership. First Kings 4 says, "Judah and Israel were as numerous as the sand by the sea in multitude, eating and drinking and rejoicing" (1 Kings 4:20). "…[They] had peace on every side all around," and they "dwelt safely, each man under his vine and his fig tree…" (1 Kings 4:20; 24-25).

While many Jewish people still look back on the time of David and Solomon as the Golden Age of Israel, we as believers find that it is, in fact, a look forward to the coming of the Kingdom of God in Christ. In ruling by divine wisdom, Solomon brought the nation into alignment with the government of Heaven. The peace, prosperity, rejoicing, and safety that Israel experienced are evidence that they were aligned with the Kingdom that is "righteousness, peace and joy in the Holy Spirit" (Rom. 14:17).

The relationship between David and Solomon—the generational transfer of wisdom and purpose—is a prophetic picture of Christ and the Church. David began to establish in the kingdom of Israel a foundation that involved an entirely different approach to His presence. Solomon built upon his father's foundation and brought that kingdom to a mature expression of worship and social life. Similarly, Christ, the Son of David, ushered in the

Kingdom of God, and has entrusted the Church with the commission to co-labor and co-create with the Holy Spirit to establish that Kingdom on earth as it is in Heaven.

This is the responsibility of every believer. God has given us a role that put us directly in line with Solomon when it comes to the priority of pursuing divine wisdom. He has called us to be kings and priests. (See Rev. 1:5.) This role is to *re-present* the King and His Kingdom, and in so doing, to bring earthly reality into alignment with Heaven.

The Kingdom that we represent perfectly expresses the wisdom of God. The Spirit that we co-labor with is the Spirit of Wisdom. This means that we as believers have unique access to the original design for our world as well as the power that made and sustains it.

Thus, we are carriers of the answers to every problem in the world—every way in which creation has strayed from God's original intent. Christ declared, "The kingdom of God is within you" (Luke 17:21). Our job is to establish that Kingdom around us by releasing what is in us through the demonstration of divine wisdom. The apostle Paul describes the Church's commission to display the wisdom of God in Ephesians 3:8-12:

> *To me, who am less than the least of all the saints, this grace was given, that I should preach among the Gentiles the unsearchable riches of Christ, and to make all see what is the fellowship of the mystery, which from the beginning of the ages has been hidden*

in God who created all things through Jesus Christ; to the intent that now the manifold wisdom of God might be made known by the church to the principalities and powers in the heavenly places, according to the eternal purpose which He accomplished in Christ Jesus our Lord, in whom we have boldness and access with confidence through faith in Him.

What was the eternal purpose of God that He accomplished through Christ? It was to restore mankind as sons and daughters and to our original intended role of co-ruling with Him over creation. As we become mature sons and daughters of our Father and become living models of what God *intended,* that is, of His wisdom, we enforce the victory Christ accomplished over the principalities and powers in the heavenly places.

The testimony of life in Israel under Solomon's reign should stir something in us. David and Solomon were able to access the power and wisdom released through keeping the testimony that brought the nation into a level of transformation none of us have seen.

Certainly, we who have been brought into the covenant by which the Spirit of Wisdom actually dwells within us should expect God to be very capable and willing to bring that transformation through us to the world around us. The testimony of David and Solomon exposes the perversion of thinking that our responsibility as believers in society is nothing more than taking comfort in how bad the world is getting because it's a sign that Jesus will return soon.

If God didn't care about the quality of life on this planet, then all of Jesus' miracles would have been absurd. Jesus did not comfort the blind man by telling him how great it was going to be when he would finally get to heaven and be able to see. Jesus' instructions for relationships, finances, and authority all had to do with a life influenced by Heaven in the here and now.

The testimony of David and Solomon, along with the testimony of Jesus and His Church, clearly demonstrates that our responsibility to bring transformation is not something that happens in only one generation. We are all called to have a vision for transformation that extends beyond our lifetimes. This generational vision is built into God's original commands concerning the testimony. The command in Deuteronomy 6:6-7 to teach the testimonies to our children is the first thing on the list of what we're to do in order to keep the testimony.

This proved to be one of the pillars of life for the nation of Israel. We've also seen that the writer of Psalm 78 caught the significance of this command and its power to unite the generations in a sustained relationship with God:

For He established a testimony in Jacob,
And appointed a law in Israel,
Which He commanded our fathers,
That they should make them known to their children;

That the generation to come might know them,
The children who would be born,
That they may arise and declare them to their children,
That they may set their hope in God,
And not forget the works of God,
But keep His commandments (Psalm 78:5-7).

In the legacy of David and Solomon, generations were united by the testimony. When one generation receives the inheritance of revelation in the testimonies and builds upon the foundation laid by their fathers by pursuing their own relationship with God and their responsibilities before Him, there is an exponential rate of increase in the demonstration of that revelation.

We believe in investing in the next generation so that our ceiling can become their floor. What we see with David and Solomon is that when Solomon built his floor on his father's ceiling, it went from being a one-story building to a high-rise. He could do so because the testimony that reveals God's nature was established, becoming the foundation necessary for societal transformation. When that foundation is in place, there is unlimited potential for building, as there is no greater foundation for society than the nature of God.

THE POWER OF AGREEMENT

God's entire strategy for world transformation centers on the power of agreement that is released as families produce godly offspring and walk in covenant. This strategy is based on His wisdom. Our view of history must be founded on the principles of who God is and how He works. These principles are revealed in the testimony as we fight to see a sustained transfer of revelation, impartation, and influence to the successive generations of the Church

Multi-generational revival and transformation require intentionality. In Psalm 78, the psalmist speaks of fathers, children, grandchildren, and great-grandchildren keeping the testimony. Roughly, this corresponds to a century in the life of a family.

I have decided to live with a hundred-year vision for revival and Kingdom transformation, creating a culture where the testimony influences every one of our decisions and strategies as we remember, record, talk about, teach, and study the works of God.

In our families, our goal is to train the next generation to be raised aware of the supernatural interventions of God. We take time to tell our children stories of miracles to foster hunger and expectation. We teach them the promises of what God wants to do for them. As a result, we have small children who are prophesying, healing the sick, experiencing heavenly visitations, and generally stepping into everything contained in the testimonies— now, rather than waiting until they are grown-ups.

The testimony transforms God encounters in our city as well. For example, we regularly see the prophetic power of the testimony released as people encounter individuals who need miracles and minister to them by sharing the breakthroughs others have received in similar situations. Sometimes someone will simply hear the testimony and find that God has just "done it again" for them in that very moment.

If we hear statistics about the high divorce rate or poverty in our community, we intentionally collect testimonies of healed marriages and financial breakthrough. In doing so, we arm ourselves so that when we inevitably encounter the "statistics" around us, we are ready with stories tailor-made for their situations.

But we also take time to declare these testimonies over our city. By releasing the prophetic anointing in this way, we help bring about a shift in the atmosphere. We make the places of greatest weakness and brokenness targets for the invasion of Heaven.

We've actually seen a significant economic shift take place in Redding, which was once known as "Poverty Flats," over the last decade. We felt that the Lord showed us that we were to target the spirit of poverty in our city by engaging in acts of radical generosity until it became a lifestyle. This includes everything from tipping waiters and waitresses to taking up offerings for the other churches in the city.

In other words, God wanted us to create some stories that were worth talking about. It's great when you can get unbelievers to prophesy over your city by simply giving them a testimony that they can't help but talk about.

We are currently watching the economy grow in our city in a truly remarkable way, and we know it's because the wisdom of God has been demonstrated and the testimony has been released in this particular realm of life.

Multi-generational revival, along with societal transformation (the Kingdom coming "on earth as it is in heaven"), are at the top of God's agenda. It must be what drives everything I do. Keeping the testimony releases the revelation of God's nature into the earth, which in turn releases the power of God into the specific calamities of humanity. This is what helps to sustain revival by unlocking the heavenly resources of prophetic anointing and divine wisdom. It must become the intentional focus of the church worldwide.

These convictions are the impulse for this book. I truly believe that as the revelation of the power of the testimony is released across this generation, we have the potential to shape the course of world history. We will turn our attention from what's going wrong or what isn't happening to what God wants to do, as we prophesy accordingly over individuals, cities, and nations. Such divine purpose enables us to link arms and hearts with our sons and daughters in a passionate pursuit of the God revealed through our inheritance, the testimony.

CHAPTER 9

Releasing the Presence of God

Our greatest responsibility to God and/or people is not to pursue or provide more eloquent displays of the Gospel, or even miracles. Neither is it merely to speak truth in the sense of preaching or a one-on-one witness of the Gospel. Our great responsibility is to know God and make God known. Learning how to do this effectively should capture our hearts and attention for a lifetime.

For at least 20 years, a driving force within me has been the conviction that *I owe people an encounter with God.* I owe them more than just a message filled with truth. Whatever I do for people must contain the opportunity for a divine encounter. If I am full of the Spirit, my preaching, service, and various forms of ministry will be more likely to bring people into such an encounter.

In part that is what the apostle Paul meant when he stated, "And my speech and my preaching were not with persuasive words of human wisdom, but in demonstration of the Spirit and of power" (1 Cor. 2:4). People don't need to be convinced of our insights, gifts, or ability to convey truth. These things are secondary in importance at best. What people need is God. Encountering His power is encountering Him. Paul was so convinced of this that he wanted people to put their faith in the power of God (see 1 Cor. 2:5).

LEARNING TO RELEASE

God is a God of covenant. He is confident enough and sovereign enough to bind Himself to agreements with His children. I don't like to think of them as contracts—that is much too sterile. I prefer speaking in terms of relational boundaries. As we become like Jesus through obedience, we find that obedience releases His presence, His power, and His glory. And while I don't understand it fully, He has interest in our opinions and input. He is the one who promises, "If you abide in Me, and My words abide in you, you will ask what you desire, and it shall be done for you." (See John 15:7.) It is foolish to think that He makes us robotic first and then offers us the promise, "Ask what you desire." He actually trusts those who become like His Son. In that light, it is then normal for us to long for the power of God to be displayed in lives of the broken.

God cannot be properly or even accurately represented without power. Miracles are absolutely necessary for people to see Him clearly. Testifying about these miracles is part of the debt that we owe the world. When we speak, He comes to confirm what was spoken.

He has chosen to reveal Himself through people who yield to Him. His appearances are often spectacular and dramatic, as seen throughout history. His manifestations through His people may at times be similarly amazing, yet are often practical and normal.

I often learn by accidentally stumbling onto a truth. It usually starts with seeing the fruit of something before I understand it. If you live just to obey, no matter what, this will become a way of learning for you, too. It means that you don't need to understand in order to obey.

Such obedience always brings fruit, but the fruit is designed to entice you to pursue the mystery behind it. It is acceptable not to understand Kingdom principles, as their power and effect are released through obedience. But if I don't understand them, I have less opportunity to be intentional in the release of His presence, and I am unable to train others to do the same.

The release of the presence of God, which contains the Kingdom of God, is done through five activities of which I am aware:

Laying on of hands is a biblical mandate and one of the basic doctrines of Christ (see Heb. 6:1-2). Because the Kingdom is within us, it is released through the touch of faith. It is an intentional act for healing, blessing, or impartation (Mark 16:18; 1 Tim. 4:14). It is the principle of touch and release.

Proximity to the anointing. This principle worked through the apostle Peter when the sick were placed in a location where Peter's shadow would fall upon them as he walked by.

Whatever overshadows you will be released through your shadow. The garment of Jesus fits into this category as well, for He didn't purposefully lay His hands on the woman with the issue of blood (Mark 5:28-29) or the multitudes (Mark 6:56), yet they were healed. The same applies to the articles of clothing taken from the apostle Paul (Acts 19:11-12). In each case the anointing was upon them to such a degree that even their clothing became saturated with God's miracle power.

The principle of physical location as it pertains to the anointing is crucial in releasing the Kingdom. We recently had a man with a deaf ear walk into one of our healing rooms. His ear opened the moment he walked into the room. Another deaf man had his ears open when he just walked past the same room. He entered Heaven's atmosphere on earth. This *release* of power isn't as obvious as the other four on this list, as the real intentionality on this one is in *hosting His presence* more than releasing power. But you can't get one without the other.

Acts of faith release the Kingdom, as faith requires an activity. This is one of the easiest principles to prove in Scripture. Jesus was often brought into an impossibility because of someone else's faith.

Matthew 8:10 records a story where Jesus was stunned by the incredible level of faith in the centurion. He was a high-ranking Roman soldier, not a Jew, yet his faith caught Jesus completely off guard. I love the idea of having faith that grabs God's attention, drawing Him into a situation. It takes faith to please Him, and I really want to please Him.

Prophetic acts are unusual in that the action is not related to the desired outcome, as is the act of faith. For example, Elisha heard the cries of the sons of the prophets when they lost a borrowed axe head (see 2 Kings 6). It fell into the water. Elisha had them throw a stick into the water, and the axe head floated to the surface. Wood doesn't have that effect on axe heads in the natural. It was powerful because it was an act of obedience. There was no logical connection to the recovery of the axe head, yet without it there would have been no recovery. Physical obedience brings spiritual release.

The declaration is the final area that has a primary focus of this book, for nothing happens in the Kingdom without a declaration. But when we say what the Father is saying, all of Heaven is brought into the equation. When that declaration is a testimony, we capture the momentum of the history of God's dealings with mankind. Then a creative prophetic power is released into the atmosphere to establish the revelation of God on the earth.

It is imperative that we no longer do this unintentionally or sporadically; rather, it must become the intentional strategy of a last days' army. We are to burn with the conviction that we carry the revelation of God's nature and presence for all to see. We possess such extraordinary revelations of His nature within our testimonies. What is becoming commonplace for us the world is hungry to hear.

We must focus on God's heart for the nations. The testimony, and the prophetic anointing it releases, will bring about a return of the nations to God's ordained purposes. This is the reason He has given us everything as an inheritance (John 16:15; 1 Cor. 3:21). We'll need everything to accomplish our assignment.

HEAVENLY MANDATES

There are at least four priorities the Church must embrace to fulfill God's purpose for us on the earth. These are mandates from Heaven, priorities that affect thoughts, prayers, and pursuits. They are both fruit and gifts—results of being in right standing with God and attainments received only through obedience.

Love—While faith is what's required to please God, it is *love* that remains the greatest of all virtues. Love never fails. It is perfect, totally unselfish to the point of the ultimate sacrifice, taking us to where only Jesus has gone. He loved the world so much that He gave...and it's faith that works through love. So they remain the two absolutes that are the evidence of being a true believer.

Purity—The tragedy of sinfulness within the Church has caused a domino effect out of the church. Holiness is the absolute evidence of the Gospel's effect on a life. Without it, our good intentions collapse under the weight of God's purposes on the earth. He shakes whatever has faulty foundations. And sin is the weakest foundation of all. The call to disciple nations has holiness at its foundation.

Power—It is impossible to represent God without *power*. He is not an idea, a philosophy, or a creed. He is the awesome, all-powerful God. And we have been selected as agents of that power, to confront and destroy the works of darkness in the same way that Jesus did. For Jesus is the clearest revelation of God on the earth—He is perfect theology. Now the Father wants that representation to be multiplied millions of times over through us.

Glory—This is the other mandatory element that will be spoken of more and more in these last days. It is the manifested presence of Jesus—that which radiates from the Father (see Heb. 1:3). It is the weightiness of God's presence that rests upon His people in increasing measure as we give place for Him. When His glory comes into a room, there is little else one can do except to worship. We must long for these times, pursue these times, and treasure these times as they are available to us in increasing measures.

The issue of stewardship comes into play here, as those who are faithful in little will be entrusted with much. Why is the glory so important? It is the realm of God we were created to live in.

OUR GREATEST ASSIGNMENT

Our greatest treasure is God Himself. Our greatest privilege is to manifest Him. The people of God around the world are crying out for God to show up in a more significant way. It's a healthy cry. But tragically, history is filled with those who have prayed that prayer for years without ever seeing a true visitation of God. Many of the highly respected books on revival were written by people who never took part in one.

Is it that hard to get God to show up? Jesus was born in a manger—He's not that picky. Such an absence of His manifested presence has been attributed to His sovereignty. But I think it's unfair to sweep unfulfilled promises into a category called *God's sovereignty,* where God gets blamed for any lack we experience by our just stating it was because of His mysterious ways.

The only time the disciples couldn't bring deliverance to a tormented child, they weren't content with the absence of a miracle, assuming it was God's sovereign will. And so, they asked Jesus. He demonstrated how and then told them why, and the child was set free. In other words, don't blame the Father. The lack is always on our end of the equation. The covenant is complete and effective for all.

God will allow us to carry as much of His presence as we're willing to jealously guard. It has never crossed our minds how much is available to us now. Moses, who was not even born again (because Jesus had not yet died for our sins), carried a measure of Jesus' presence that is unusual for today. That shouldn't be. Inferior covenants should not provide superior blessings. The blood of Jesus gives us access to a far greater glory than was ever experienced by Moses (see 2 Cor. 3:7-11).

HEAVEN'S ECONOMY

As previously stated, Heaven's resources are released through declaration. It is one of the reasons the testimony is so effective. Each story carries revelation of His nature and His covenant with mankind. As testimonies are spoken, something is released and created. The resources of His world are released into this one.

Jesus is the Word of God made flesh. When Jesus spoke, His words were spirit (John 6:63). We are called to speak words that impact the reality around us. When we say what the Father is saying, we cause Heaven to affect those who hear. Our words become spirit in the same way as the words of Jesus did, and so they impact the world around us. There's never been a more important time for us to hear from God that we might speak what He speaks and alter the nature of the world we live in.

Please take notice that God manifests through words. Not only is there life and death in the power of our speech, but He Himself also rides upon our words when they originate in the Father's heart. Hearing the words that come from His heart must be the passion of every believer. For in hearing His voice, faith is born, and the release of God's presence is imminent. I can't think of a greater responsibility or privilege.

MULTI-GENERATIONAL PROMISE

One of the Psalms mentioned earlier in this book carries unique revelation for us. It is Psalm 78. It contains some of the most startling promises and warnings in the Bible. Included in these verses is the insight needed to keep a generation from rebellion while cultivating in them a heart of loyalty to God.

> *We will not hide them from their children,*
> *Telling to the generation to come the praises of the*
> *Lord,*
> *And His strength and His wonderful works that He*
> *has done.*
> *For He established a testimony in Jacob,*
> *And appointed a law in Israel,*
> *Which He commanded our fathers,*
> *That they should make them known to their*
> *children;*
> *That the generation to come might know them,*
> *The children who would be born,*
> *That they may arise and declare them to their*
> *children,*
> *That they may set their hope in God,*
> *And not forget the works of God,*
> *But keep His commandments;*
> *And may not be like their fathers,*
> *A stubborn and rebellious generation,*

A generation that did not set its heart aright,
And whose spirit was not faithful to God (Psalm 78:4-8).

This psalm carries wonderful insights of the purpose and outcome of embracing the testimony—that which releases the reality of God into a generation. The effect of neglect is also frighteningly obvious.

The record of God's activities among men is not to be hidden or forgotten. It must be declared to the younger generation, who must in turn be trained to do the same with their own children. The chain must not be broken. It is one of increasing revelation of God's nature and presence upon the earth. Each generation is privileged to build upon the previous one, until the manifestation of God's nature and presence becomes more and more pronounced.

The nations that surrounded Israel in the wilderness saw the presence and glory of God upon them. That should not be the *high water mark* for God manifesting Himself upon His people. The blood of Jesus qualifies us for more!

The promised result is the cry of every believing family—that our youth would set their hope in God! Notice the role that remembering God's works plays in establishing a firm footing for an entire generation. This one act shapes culture more than most of the things we often pour ourselves into: things that have little lasting result.

Yet this ancient boundary—keeping the testimony— actually impacts the consciousness, priorities, and mind-sets of an entire generation. The works of God become the single greatest culture-shaping element in the King-dom. There are very few things in Scripture that carry that kind of promised impact. The psalmist takes it a step further: if God's people will embrace their responsibility with the testimony, they can prevent rebellion and destroy stubbornness.

By not keeping the testimony as a divine charge, Israel ended up in the ultimate sin of unbelief. "In spite of this, *they still sinned, and did not believe in His wondrous works*" (Ps. 78:32). Faith is natural for those who embrace the record of God's activities among mankind. It is the equivalent of Jesus' comment to the Pharisees when He said, "But you do not have His word abiding in you, because whom He sent, Him you do not believe" (John 5:38).

When we hold what is valuable to God in our hearts, we are prepared to believe when Jesus steps onto the scene. The testimony plays that role. Sin was inevitable as they lost contact with His works and their hearts became hard.

God does not like to be confined. "Yes, again and again *they tempted God, and limited the Holy One* of Israel" (Ps. 78:41). *Putting restraints on the revelation of God's nature is foolish at best. Israel had made a habit of limiting God.* He was again confined in Nazareth and didn't like it. Nazareth was the one place where the nature of God was not presented as the Father intended (see Mark 6:6).

Faith pleases God; unbelief causes Him grief, and is at the root of betrayal as seen with the Judas spirit (see John 6:64). The New American Standard Bible translates the Hebrew word for *limited* this way: they caused God *pain*, which is very similar to the New Testament command, "Do not grieve the Holy Spirit" (Eph. 4:30). All acts of obedience are to come out of our relationship with the Holy Spirit.

They did not remember His power:
The day when He redeemed them from the enemy,
When He worked His signs in Egypt,
And His wonders in the field of Zoan (Psalm 78:42-43).

Yet they tested and provoked the Most High God,
And did not keep His testimonies (Psalm 78:56).

When we fail to remember God's works, disaster is imminent. Many can remember stories of God's interventions, if asked. But few keep them at the forefront of their thinking and conversation. The neglect of this one truth is at the heart of the collapse of the Church of power. The record of the release of God's power on the earth is an anchor for our souls. With it at the forefront of our minds, our ambitions and pursuits become eternal in effect. Without it, we are boats tossed by the waves of chaotic spiritual environments.

The promise given at the beginning of this psalm was that the upcoming generation could be kept from rebellion if their parents would fulfill their role in keeping the testimony, speaking the testimony, and training the next generation what to do with this great inheritance that reveals God's nature and presence.

In verse 56 of Psalm 78, we see the alternative—"provoking" God or rebellion results in the absence of the ultimate reference point for life—God's nature. And that nature is revealed in the testimony. Ignoring it is sailing without a compass.

There is a powerful momentum created when entire communities build a culture around keeping the testimony, as well as dire consequences that develop when the testimony is forgotten on the same scale.

But chose the tribe of Judah,
Mount Zion which He loved.
And He built His sanctuary like the heights,
Like the earth which He has established forever.
He also chose David His servant,
And took him from the sheepfolds;
From following the ewes that had young He brought
him,
To shepherd Jacob His people,
And Israel His inheritance.
So he shepherded them according to the integrity of
his heart,

And guided them by the skillfulness of his hands
(Psalm 78:68-72).

This is an unusual end to a psalm that carries such strong warning about neglecting the works of God. Out of nowhere, it seems, David is brought into the picture. It may appear awkward at first, until we remember that no one in Scripture embraced the *culture-shaping value* of the testimony as did David. They were his counselors, his meditation at night, his pursuit in study, and his inheritance. Testimonies were so important that he made sure that Solomon, the son that would be king, was groomed on this diet.

It is also no mistake that the one known for a life of worship was so extremely devoted to living under the influence of the works of God. When you see the wonder of God through His works, you can't help but become the living offering in worship.

What can we learn from the conclusion to this psalm? Israel had occasional success and much failure. Their success seemed to depend on the integrity of those in charge. While there were other righteous leaders in Israel's history besides David, none made the impact, according to the principles of grace found in the New Testament, that he did.

The introduction of David in this psalm reminds us that more than any leader in history, he represents a heavenly culture—the kind that great kingdoms are known for. His example was the answer for the continual failings of a people who throughout this psalm had lost their sense of purpose and direction, both of which had been reinforced by their history of God's supernatural interventions.

David's abandonment in worship represented his affinity to the realities of Heaven permeating his life. That is the nature of the life of one who lives to release the power of that world into this one.

HISTORY PROPHESIES

On July 17, 1859, Charles Spurgeon brought forth a message entitled, "The Story of God's Mighty Acts." One hundred and fifty years ago, he declared this truth that had the power to shape the culture of the Church until there was a full restoration of God's historic interventions among mankind. Listen to his prophetic cry:

> When people hear about what God used to do, one of the things they say is: "Oh, that was a very long while ago." ... I thought it was God that did it. Has God changed? Is he not an immutable God, the same yesterday, today and forever? Does not that furnish an argument to prove that what God has done at one time he can do at another? Nay, I think I may push it a little further, and say *what he has done once, is a prophecy of what he intends to do again.... Whatever God has done...is to be looked upon as a precedent....* [Let us] with earnestness seek that God would restore to us the faith of the men of old, that we may richly enjoy his grace as in the days of old.

In 1859, through this great prophetic preacher, the chance was given to initiate a full recovery of all that had been lost. History tells us the Church did little with this truth, except perhaps to applaud another great sermon. We are now presented with a similar opportunity.

In a relay race there are four runners. The first three do not leave the racetrack and go into the showers before the last one finishes the race, because they all receive a prize according to how the last runner finishes. At this moment the *cloud of witnesses* are waiting to see what we will do with what we've been given (see Heb. 12:1). Let's not miss our opportunity to see a full restoration of God's works with mankind until Jesus is accurately *re-presented* and His glory fills the earth. This must happen through the obedience of a generation who captures the momentum of history through *keeping the testimony, thereby fully releasing the power of Jesus.*

ENDNOTE

1. http://www.spurgeon.org/sermons/0263.htm.

Author Contact Information

Bill Johnson
Bethel Church
933 College View Drive
Redding, CA 96003

Website: www.iBethel.org
www.BillJohnsonMinistries.com

Ministry Resources

How to Overcome Disappointment
2 CD Set

The Christian life is the life of short accounts that don't allow unresolved disappointment to fill the heart. When what God said abides in the believer's heart, it prepares the believer to hear when God speaks a divine invitation into the impossible.

By contending in weakness and disappointment, God is proclaiming promises into our lives, unveiling our stewardship of past disappointments, and qualifying what we will carry in the future.

Mission Possible
Single CD

God gave us the impossible assignment to disciple nations. Within that command is the enablement to see it performed. Through examples of recent events of heavenly invasions, this teaching ignites the listener to the awareness of how close Heaven is. God opens this inheritance to the Church to give understanding and access, to know that we already posses that which attracts the outpouring. Be stirred as you turn your heart to Heaven, inviting His presence to come even more.

Revolution: Erasing the Lines Between the Secular and the Sacred
Single CD

When the believer comes into the Kingdom, there is no such thing as a secular part of his or her life; everything becomes purposeful. God is leveling the playing field of the Kingdom, where the businessman, school teacher, stay-at-home mom and wife—the "ministers of the Gospel"—live with significance to shape the course of worldwide history. By giving a complete yes to God, they step into a role of living on the edge of what God is doing, making it the center of what is to come.

Healing: Our Neglected Birthright
6 CD Set

Any area of a person's life that is not under the influence of hope is under the influence of a lie, and hope is the atmosphere in which faith grows. It is natural for a Christian to hunger to see impossibilities bow at the name of Jesus because we are a people born to confront and reverse the works of the devil. This series is a practical tool to discover the full provision of the Cross and how Jesus has enabled us to be successful in fulfilling His mandate.

The Advancing Kingdom: A Practical Guide to the Normal Christian Life of Victory and Purpose
4 CD Set

The strategies of hell are to distract and derail us from God's agenda through accusations and intimidation. The safest place for the believer is not in defending what we have, but in positioning ourselves for advancement. It is the sacrificial lifestyle that creates an atmosphere around believers that insulates us from the destructive tactics of the devil and enables us to walk in increasing victory and joy.

Leading From the Heart
8 CD Set

God has raised up true leaders the same way for centuries—with training that begins with the heart. Skills can be learned, but a Christ-like heart comes through repentance, discipline, and encounters with God Himself. Our faithfulness in these areas determines how much authority we can be trusted with. This series addresses the multifaceted characteristics of leaders who walk in loyalty, grace, wisdom, and most importantly, with a value, above all, for the Presence.

The Quest for the Face of God
4 CD Set

Our initial response to God is our salvation, yet the "quest" lies within our ultimate response to seek and experience His face. He is the center. As we experience the face of God, we discover a new identity outpouring of influence and favor that empowers us to change the course of history. Join the quest—it is all-consuming and glorious beyond description.

From Glory to Glory: Biblical Patterns for Sustaining Revival
4 CD Set

Every believer has the responsibility to carry revival as if he or she were the only one responsible. God's manifest presence and favor marked the Church of Acts with uncompromising standards, which caused the message of the Church to increase in its power and demonstration.

This message illustrates how Kingdom increase is the calculated devotion to a move of God, exposing some of the tests that prove our readiness for more and how we capture the favor and attention of Heaven through a lifestyle of faithfulness and honor.

Recommend Reading

A Life of Miracles by Bill Johnson

Basic Training for the Prophetic Ministry by Kris Vallotton

Basic Training for the Supernatural Ways of Royalty by Kris Vallotton

Developing a Supernatural Lifestyle by Kris Vallotton

Dreaming With God by Bill Johnson

Face to Face by Bill Johnson

Here Comes Heaven by Bill Johnson and Mike Seth

Loving Our Kids on Purpose by Danny Silk

Purity—The New Moral Revolution by Kris Vallotton

Strengthen Yourself in the Lord by Bill Johnson

The Happy Intercessor by Beni Johnson

The Supernatural Power of a Transformed Mind by Bill Johnson

The Supernatural Ways of Royalty by Kris Vallotton and Bill Johnson

The Ultimate Treasure Hunt by Kevin Dedmon

When Heaven Invades Earth by Bill Johnson